S0-AGQ-273

Her effort to create portraits of a woman's journey is beautifully successful. She paints images with words that stir deep emotions. Her descriptions reach inside and grab your heart and gut before they ever travel to your mind. I was moved over and over again.
—Paula D'Arcy,
Author, *Song for Sarah* and *Gift of the Red Bird*

We see ourselves in these stories through the eyes of a most careful observer. In many local colors Joy Jordan-Lake goes beyond gender, race, and generation to what is most humorous and human and sacred within us.
—Kelly K. Monroe,
Editor, *Finding God at Harvard*
Founder, The Harvard Veritas Forum

Grit&Grace

PORTRAITS OF A WOMAN'S LIFE

Joy Jordan-Lake

Harold Shaw Publishers
Wheaton, Illinois

Though characters in the fiction pieces may be based on actual persons, none are meant to be true representations and should be noted as fiction.

The following pieces have been previously published and here appear in edited form:

"Peanut Butter on Fine China, French Wine in a Paper Cup" first appeared under the title "Jesus Makes Me Nervous" in *The Christian Century* (July 27–August 3, 1994). Used by permission.

"When Johnnie Sue Got Religion" first appeared in *Prism* (May/June 1995). Used by permission.

"Crusader in Floral Print" reprinted from *MissionsUSA* (Vol.65, No.4), © The Home Mission Board of the Southern Baptist Convention. All rights reserved. Used by permission.

Copyright © 1997 by Joy Jordan-Lake

All rights reserved. No part of this book may be reproduced or transmitted in any form or by any means, electronic or mechanical, including photocopying, recording, or any information storage and retrieval system, without written permission from Harold Shaw Publishers, Box 567, Wheaton, Illinois 60189. Printed in the United States of America.

Unless otherwise noted, Scripture quotations are taken from the *New Revised Standard Version of the Bible,* © 1989 by the Division of Christian Education of the National Council of the Churches of Christ in the United States of America, and are used by permission. All rights reserved.

Scripture quotations marked (NIV) are taken from the HOLY BIBLE, NEW INTERNATIONAL VERSION®. Copyright © 1973, 1978, 1984 International Bible Society. Used by permission of Zondervan Publishing House. All rights reserved.

ISBN 0-87788-738-1

Cover design by David LaPlaca

Library of Congress Cataloging-in-Publication Data

Jordan-Lake, Joy, 1963-
   Grit and grace : portraits of a woman's life / Joy Jordan-Lake.
     p. cm.
   ISBN 0-87788-738-1
   1. Women—Literary collections. 2. Women. I. Title.
  PS3560.07645G75 1997
  818'.5409—dc21   96-54587
                                   CIP

04 03 02 01 00 99 98 97
10 9 8 7 6 5 4 3 2 1

For my mother,
 Diane Owen Jordan,
and my daughter,
 Julia Jordan-Lake:
How much I learn from both of you!

Contents

Acknowledgments

It's important to me to have a chance to say *thanks*

. . . To Todd Lake, my husband and my friend, whose abundant encouragement, support, and love help me grow, personally and professionally. (Though I would get far more writing done if I enjoyed talking with, working with, and laughing with you less!)

. . . And to Julia, our precious daughter, whose accommodating sleep schedule has taught me self-discipline and focus as nothing else could. What a delight you are every day!

. . . To Diane and Monty Jordan, my own mom and dad, who, through the examples set in their own creative and spiritual lives, impressed upon us kids early the centrality of words, and in particular the *Word incarnate,* in all the mystery and impossibility those two words entail. Thanks, too, for putting up with, and not entirely curbing, my nasty stubborn streak: I've needed it a great deal lately to stay put at the computer.

. . . And to David Jordan and Beth Jackson-Jordan (and kids), Gina Lake (especially during the final week of revisions!), Steven Lake, and the (vast!) California clan, particularly the Philbin females, for being as supportive—and fun—a family as anyone could hope for.

. . . To friends on Signal Mountain, Tennessee, in the Tufts University English Department (particularly Joe Hurka and the other veteran writers) and at Cambridgeport Church in Cambridge, Massachusetts, as well as individuals who shouldn't go without a mention by name: Carol Chapman, Elizabeth and Pete Cernoia (and Micah too), Laura Singleton, Anne Moore, Kitty Freeman, Man Wah Tan, Stephanie Powers, Peter Choo, Gloria White-Hammond, Kelly Monroe, the Bothwell family, Susan Bahner Lancaster and family, Cherry

Foreman, Larry Woiwode, Jean MacPhee, Rose Phillips, and Barbara Bell King. All of you contributed significantly (whether knowingly or not) to this collection, either by brainstorming on book titles, by timely encouragements, by sharing an interest in writing, by living your lives in ways that inspire, by simple, unshakeable friendship—or all of the above.

. . . To Ginger and Milton Brasher-Cunningham for their love, loyalty, and wisdom, as well as for the inspiration for two of the pieces in this collection. The chapter "Created to Dance" was written for Ginger's installation as associate pastor of First Congregational, Winchester.

The chapter "Prodigal" was written to be read in conjunction with Milton's performing the song "Come and See," composed by Milton and Billy Crockett (to be found on Billy's album *Red Bird, Blue Sky,* a magnificent piece of musicianship and theological reflection).

. . . To Mrs. Buckshorn, my fifth-grade teacher, who, long before I'd ever told anyone what I wanted to do when I grew up, gave me an article on authors and their first books "for when you are a writer one day."

. . . And to Lil Copan, the editor without whom this book would not be. Period.

Introduction

Gather together any group of women and whatever else results from the mix you will most certainly get *stories:* stories of twenty-eight-minute labors and the child who crowned in that single step between the hospital sidewalk and a speeding car *(. . . So here I am having a baby in my sweatpants and Joe's yellin' to me, "Hon, do we have money for parking?");* stories such as fisherman tell, only far fewer of the One That Got Away than of the One That Got Tossed Back *(. . . Girl, I'm telling you, that man wouldn't make good shark feed);* stories of coming to terms with the way we view our own bodies *(. . . I was walking back from the ladies' room the long way and feeling good, thinking how all these heads are turning, everybody's looking at me, and I'm thinking how much more than just good I must be looking, 'til I get to my seat and see my skirt's hiked up in my pantyhose clear up to my waist).*

Stories are how we initiate the young *(. . . Now wearing white shorts is to that time of the month as not carrying an umbrella is to rain: you're just asking for a downpour, like the time I . . .).* Stories are how we share the excitement of a budding relationship *(. . . We first met when he crossed the street to complain about my dog—imagine the nerve—who barked incessantly, yes, but whose manners otherwise were vastly superior to most people's),* as well as warn of the work ahead *(. . . It was along about the year the roof and the pipes had to be replaced that I guess we started wondering about replacing each other—gotten real worn out, what we had, with too many holes to want to keep patching up).*

Stories are how women communicate best, how we explain and entertain, how we caution—and celebrate.

A reader once looked at some short stories I'd

11

written a couple of years before. In them she noted what she described as an overriding theme of hostility towards men. I was startled, unaware of any such theme in myself. When I reported that reader's analysis to a close friend, she reminded me of my frustrations at the time working as a part-time pastor, still a predominantly male profession. My friend, who is also a trained counselor, could not be induced to discuss the stories' literary merit or lack thereof; rather, "What great therapy!" was her conclusion.

True enough. For me, for all of us, our stories are therapy. And healing. A first swat at trying to fight back—or maybe forgive. A first release of long-clutched anger. A final step towards embrace.

Our stories are a way of asking, *Is this something I should feel as badly about as I do?* A way of holding hands over long-distance lines and throwing confetti that no one will have to sweep up later; a way of shouting, *So bully for us—we did it!* Our stories can be a way of saying to our mothers, *Part of what I am is who you are,* a way of teaching us about ourselves even as we tell the tales: reminding us where we've come from, empowering us for who we are becoming. Women's stories, the stories of the journey through our lives—told and re-told, howled over, snickered over, wept over—when gathered together, form a party to which grit and grace, strength from within and strength from without, arrive hand in hand.

A colleague, expressing interest in this collection in its early stages, asked me, "Are they your stories? Are they true stories?" Yes and yes, I suppose. Yes, they are my stories, some from my own life and some from the lives of women around me—and therefore mine too: if we care anything for justice and compassion and mercy and love, the stories of any one become the stories of us all. And yes, the stories are true, in that any story of pain or struggle or delight anchored in real life is always true, whether it is historical fact or fact fictionalized. This collection contains both. I hope that these stories, *our* stories, accurately reflect something of the female experience in all its humor and heartache—and wonder.

Over the years I have watched and I have listened—to my own life as a girl, as a single adult, as a wife, as a mother, as a professional, and to the beautifully, painfully, marvelously complex lives of the women around me. The following are portraits and sketches of women whose stories are genuine, though in some cases altered for privacy's sake (settings shifted or different women's stories conflated). The women are not famous; do not look for them among lists of college founders and CEOs of Fortune 500 Companies or on the cover of *Time*. It is, in fact, precisely in their quite ordinary life struggles for balance, in their very typical mis-steps and recoveries, that we may find extraordinary hope.

And reason to celebrate.

Created to Dance

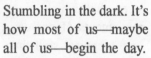

Stumbling in the dark. It's how most of us—maybe all of us—begin the day.

Never quite sure how our feet get from a warm bed to a cold floor, we find them, to our surprise and dismay, scuffling across the bedroom towards the bathroom, stubbing themselves on the dresser, tripping over the dog, and picking up splinters from the hardwood floor along the way. We begin the day by stumbling and proceed from there, gaining speed, but all too often not grace, and finally succeed only in going through the motions of a day—of a life—that really matters.

We go tripping from dilemmas at work to conflicts at home. Slipping from crashed hard drives to dented fenders. Sliding from complaining clients to crying children. Spinning from car keys we misplaced today to relationships we're losing fast. We sidestep issues we know deserve our time and become entangled by those we know do not. We bow to the wrong priorities and collapse under the wrong pressures, and glide through our own weariness in a whirl of too-loose fan belts and faulty software and jeans that weren't quite so tight last week.

We flail about in gestures that we hope look like compassion. We dash about at a rate we hope might convey we care—or would, if we only had time. Maybe next week won't be so crazy. Next week, we'll be there.

But next week, the debris of this week will hang about our ankles, will pull at our feet and trip us up and slow us down. And when it comes down to what really matters, most—maybe all—of our scuffling and spinning and sidestepping is nothing but unsynchronized, meaningless motion. So we end our days as we began them, by stumbling in the dark.

Unless we learn new steps. New sequences. New ways of maneuvering in the dim blur of a new day—our eyes still half closed from sleep.

Every now and then it happens by chance: illumination, revelation, a way of living that is something more than mere survival, a way of attending to the duties of the day that becomes itself a form of art. We find ourselves moving alone without fear, and side by side without suspicion, extending our hands beyond self-interest, stepping forward with a sure-footedness that is new, yet somehow strangely familiar. Grace has put a certain symmetry and beauty and purpose in our motions; grace has put significance in our steps. And we learn to leap for the sheer joy of knowing the Giver of Grace.

We of the human race—and maybe, just maybe, we women in particular—live clumsily in meaningless, harried existences because we were not created for them. We were intended to circle away from self-loathing and self-doubt and self-focus and lift one another up with a strength that's not our own; we were intended to help one another leap without fear, intended to hold hands and stand on our toes and look chaos and brutality and apathy in the face . . . and dance them down.

For we were created to dance. To spell out in our steps that which gives beauty and meaning to the movements of our days. To find stability less in our own technical skill than in the grace of God that balances the unsteady first position, forgives the nasty spills.

Often, though, we need someone to recall for us what it is we are supposed to be doing here: that we were created not to stumble in the dark but to dance in the light that leaves no shadow. For we are meant to be not only dancers but also teachers of the dance. Meant to come alongside and remind one another that though my steps and your steps and her steps and theirs need not follow the same pattern, still, stumbling is *not* what we—any of us—do best.

Many of us—maybe most of us—begin our days in confusion, in clumsiness. But from there we are invited to something better, something tougher, something far more beautiful. There can be more stillness, more meaning in our steps than the frantic twists of bodies jerked in thirty thousand different directions. There can be something sacred in the most faltering and the most grand of our performances.

For we are called to courage and to strength and to endurance, called to execute our lives with the grit and the grace that is ours for the taking—from the God who flings out the billowing skirts of the earth . . . and dances.

A Prayer for Our Daughters

Tonight in the storm I thaw my feet by the fire, the wood stove
serving us well, and pray that my child will always be
warm. Twenty inches, they say, surely ending
by noon. The snow will brush
the dog's tummy tomorrow—no, higher. She
likes it like that and leaps for the stick that sinks
deep into white and is lost. Golden body a blade, she drops head-
first into drifts, plowing furrows of froth, and emerges, her muzzle a beard.

My daughter laughs at her dog, baby's arms flailing high,
and her face smiles itself into knots. All she knows of the
snow is beauty and light, the dog's beard, and Daddy
tasting of salt: it takes time to shovel the drive.

But of snow caging cars, making dangerous rides
of less-traveled routes, of cold, inconvenience, of threat,
of that snow she knows nothing yet. So I pray that my daughter
will always be safe. And warm. And well loved. Though I know I must

Pray too she'll live well aware, understanding that everyone's not,
not warm and not safe and not loved. So may she live
to laugh much, yet be still willing to weep
where God's sorrow is stamped on pain.
May long life be hers too, strands of wonder and awe,
happy years strung together in a life of great worth. Yet
more crucially still, may the days she spends living count well,
not for what she's collected, bank-vaulted, but for what she has given away.

May she be healthy, God, too: show her body respect, know her parts
were hand knitted by you. But may she never neglect to nurture
her soul, which can wither, and rot, without notice.
Make her lovely with delight
in life's laughs at itself: the dog's sideburns and beard
made of snow. If my daughter is pretty, God, save her from self,
from gauging success by the heads she makes turn. May she understand
beauty's a slippery base on which to build futures, construct lives of ideals.

May her ways speak of hope in midwinter's despair, offer courage
for long journeys home. Let her practice the mixing of mercy
with strength, and power that knows how to kneel.
May her intellect thrive; may she be well read;
but may the life of the mind never numb her from feeling
the world can for some be cold. May her battles be few and
worth fighting—poverty, bigotry, pain. But in the midst of the struggle,
the close of each day, may real comfort be hers in good coffee . . . and grace.

May she never know hunger, material need; may she always thirst
for truth. Let her revere nature and in it find quiet, and reckless
communion with peace. May her passions have substance,
have heart behind words, not easily blown into heaps
by the breeze like bed sheets off the line. But her doubts,
may she face them and fearlessly test them; for belief is not blind,
nor faith without thought; no answer is injured by wondering why—
though the real cannot always be measured, nor the certain always seen.

The snow's made soft mounds of the mailbox, the shrubs. The big
dog, unbearded, drips, droops at our feet, and my daughter
is rubbing her eyes. She kicks and she wiggles
to shake off sleep's touch that would pull

her away from play. But the logs in the stove shift about,
settle in, and the dog starts to snore as the silence wraps round
us in rest. Stretching day from her body, my daughter dozes at last.
I hold her tight by the fire, and I pray. . . . I pray that she'll always be warm.

ON ADOLESCENCE

Hips and Things

She's a cartwheel dis-
   rupted, a giggle prolonged,
      a dance step just being learned.
Long legs, unshaved, last spring skipping with grace,
      today cross the classroom like
Stilts, someone else's, too large, and her face

Is like that of the dolls (her mother's, then
   handed
      down)
One summer she left out in the rain:
      bisque cheeks, splotched and spotted,
Hair, dull brass, matted, leonine mane

Cut too short for her jaw shape, too
  long
    for her brow,
A mouth set on punitive rack
  Where her teeth, crowded tusks, are confined for
    the time
In the hopes of their not moving back, while

Her hips have
  spread
    first, her chest still be-
Hind, and always two sizes too small.
  She's still blushing from buying her very first bra:
A trauma. She'd said then, if all

Of the money in all the
  wide
    world
Were hers to keep and to spend,
  She'd buy a far island to hide herself on
'Til age twelve had come to an end.

Prodigal

A woman—you might know her—had two daughters. There came a time when the younger one said to the mother just what the mother had been expecting (not looking forward to, you understand, but expecting nevertheless) to hear.

"Look," said the girl, "I need the Visa and the keys to the Volvo. And I've been meaning to mention, Mom, it's time we talked early inheritance. Here's how it is: I'd like to see this dusty old town in nothing but my long-term memory. Need a place that's got more to offer on Sunday mornings than Baptist preachers and monster truck pulls, a place where banjo's not the only beat to move to. But I've got this cash-flow problem, see, and people say *you've* got more money than God. And I figured if you divided the estate . . . So what about it, hmm?"

The woman was ready with her answer—it wasn't like she hadn't been prepared. Still, it wasn't easy. Never had been, handling this one, her youngest, her baby.

Now the two daughters of the woman, both by their looks and by the way they lived, struck everyone who knew them as having little in common. "Different from each other," the small town's Baptist preacher once described them, "as grape juice is from strong wine." And though he never made quite clear which was which, everybody figured they knew what he meant.

The older daughter was born saddle broken,

people said: tame from the start. Kind of kid who took the trash out without being asked, made her bed each morning with her sheets in tight-tucked hospital corners, saved all her nickels from the lemonade stand to give to foreign missions—and that was her rebellious stage. She grew up to drive the speed limit in a brown four-door sedan, sold life insurance, and kept a King James Bible on her desk *and* her dashboard.

"Like everybody in town didn't already know," said the younger daughter of the older, "she was up to her nose hairs in religion."

But the younger daughter had her own uses for the Good Book. They say she rolled the minor prophets into funny little cigarettes. Drove a big black Jeep with a canvas top and, when it rained, used Ezra, Nehemiah, Esther, and Job to plug up the leaks. Jeremiah made fifty-two real fine spit wads, she said, and she found that by copying off long passages of Song of Solomon, signing her name to them, and passing them out in Sunday school, she could get herself invited not to come back anymore.

"I was merely," she told her mother, "dispersing the Word of God."

The younger daughter had a certain reputation for wearing her nails too long and her skirts too short and her shirts too tight, styling her sophistication from the pages of *Cosmopolitan*. Ran around her sleepy little town like a cat with her tail caught fire.

"She dates the kind of boys," said the older daughter of the younger, "who chew tobacco for a living." And everybody figured she was being generous.

In the younger daughter's high school senior English class they'd read a seventeenth-century poem she'd liked:

Gather ye rosebuds while ye may,
Old time is still a-flying:
And this same flower that smiles today
Tomorrow will be dying. . . .

It was Robert Herrick's "To the Virgins, To Make Much of Time," and while the younger daughter wasn't still technically part of the target audience, she'd thought the poet had a point: better to wear the latest fashions while she could still fit in them, and lots of makeup . . . before she needed it.

"Better to let the boys wait in line while *their*

time," she said, failing to notice she was spilling red nail polish on her sister's sedan upholstery, "is still at *my* disposal."

A woman had two daughters. When the younger one asked for half the inheritance, her mother gave her what she wanted.

"No more flea-bitten farming town for me! Big city, here I come," said the younger daughter to the cosmetology consultants at Beautyrama down the street. "Make me classy, girls!"

So they painted the long red nails a subtler Sun-Kissed Coral, chopped the bushy mane to a bob, tamped down the bangs a bit and covered up some cleavage.

"Boston," said the younger daughter, "must be an awfully stuffy old town. But then . . . ," she cheered herself, "it hasn't yet met me!"

Away she went, dizzy with the scent of new money, to a far, far country from the land that had been her home. They say she landed at Logan Airport with a limo to meet her, and she left for downtown in a cloud of pleated silk and pink champagne. Had lunch at Four Seasons and dinner at Park Plaza. Caught a show at the Huntington, and by midnight she'd moved all fifteen pieces of matching leather luggage into the Ritz on Newbury Street—"to find out what the world is all about," she said, "and all the ways it wants to make me happy."

A woman had two daughters, and the younger one moved away. For the longest time the mother heard nothing from her. Oh, rumors now and then wound their way back home: she'd been seen here, wearing this, doing that, going there with an assortment of fine-looking fellows who worked as lawyers and bankers and legislators for a living. And then nothing. Absolutely nothing for so long the folks back home started taking bets on whether she'd end up as the first base bag at Fenway Park.

Well, winter came and went and so did spring. Then summer lumbered away too, looking back over its shoulder for a day here and there, but finally chased off by a machete-edged wind and trees with war paint on their faces.

The week the radiators, smelling of dust and disuse, came clanging, banging on for the first time, a Greyhound bus stopped in front of Beautyrama. The younger daughter spilled out of the bus, smelling to high heaven, like she'd been marinated in Jim Beam and left for dead in a camp latrine. And looking worse. Came limping down the road, almost crawling . . . when her momma saw her coming.

The woman came busting out of that house with her blue bathrobe flapping in the breeze. Lost one fuzzy slipper on the doormat and the other by the mailbox.

The younger daughter started in saying she was looking for a job as a maid or maybe a landscape assistant or a stable hand. But even those jobs, she said, were too good. Then she fell to her knees. "I really just came by to let you know I'm not dead—not quite. Not yet. Got the living soul kicked out of me, but for some reason I just haven't yet quit sucking air. Didn't have what it took to jump off the Tobin Bridge, though I tried. Hard. Twice."

"My child," said the woman.

"*No. Listen to me,*" said the girl to the woman. "When I ran out of cash I stole what I could. Then I sold all I had, piece by piece. I was still out of money . . . so I started on me."

"My child," said the woman.

"Don't call me that, *ever,*" said the girl to the woman. "See, I sold all of me, one piece at a time, some pieces so many times over 'til I'd sold my insides. All. Nothing left. Look close now. Look close at what once was your daughter—now a creature without a soul or a mind or a heart or a body to call her own."

"My child," said the woman. "You must be thirsty—"

"You're not listening to me!" cried the girl, and she sprang to her feet and clutched the woman's face with long, filthy fingernails, once manicured mauve. The girl held the face and shook it and clawed it 'til blood ran off the woman's cheeks. *"Listen to me. Don't you understand what I am?"*

"I was listening," said the woman quietly, wiping blood from her face. "I believe you are what you've said: a drunkard. And a thief. And a whore—*my child.* You must be hungry—"

The girl collapsed on the pavement, just crumpled right there, grabbed for the bathrobe and tore at its terry cloth, tore hard. "You cannot know, you cannot imagine . . . !" said the girl to the woman. "Listen to me! *I am not your child.* I don't deserve—"

"Deserve!" said the woman. *"Deserve?* And just

when, I'd like to know, have I *ever* mentioned *deserving?* See, I bore you with a pain you cannot know, you cannot imagine. You have wet in my lap and thrown up in my arms. You have cried on my shoulder and kicked at my shins. You have wrecked my car and rearranged my schedule, and your most recent decisions have ripped great holes in my heart. But if you think your slicing yourself into little pieces and selling two for a penny at Park Street Station changes now who you are, then you haven't paid much attention all these years. So now I'm asking you, if you're ready to hear, *are you thirsty?"*

A woman had two daughters, and the younger one collapsed, just crumbled, right there on the pavement in the middle of a public road. She cried into her mother's bathrobe and wiped her nose on its sleeve. Cried, and laughed some too, because life no longer made sense. The younger daughter had seen the ways of the world now; she knew how it worked. Nothing ran by these rules, not bistros, not boyfriends, not hotels, not schools. Nobody let you in, let you close, let you be a part of them without a price. The younger daughter had seen the world. And this was not it.

"Then I'm not," said the girl, holding tight to the hem of the blue bathrobe, ". . . unwelcome . . . here?"

The strength that lay beneath the blue bathrobe pulled the girl to her feet and spun her around 'til she could hardly breathe. "We'll have a party," said the woman, "hire a band, roll back the rug, call the neighbors, *celebrate!* But first, let's see about you. Come and eat."

"Eat?" said the girl weakly, looking as though she'd not allowed herself to think that thought for the longest time.

"Come and eat; come and drink; come and rest," said the woman, taking the girl by the hand.

"Rest?" said the girl, wondering now if the big goose-down comforter with pink daisies still lay on her bed.

"Come and rest; come and dance; come and play!"

"Play?" said the daughter. "Mother, please. Really. I'm grown now. Been out on my own for some time now."

"I can see that . . . , my child. Welcome home. Come and see."

The Blue Hole and the Burning Cross

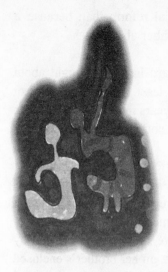

Sacred was not a word Molly Ann Maynard used much—evoking as it did images of inferior organ music, the celesta stop stuck open, and aging soprano soloists with quivering necks, the skin hanging in gathers like parlor drapes from their jaws. But some things—and some places—just are, she'd have admitted, just are sacred. The Blue Hole was that kind of place. Maybe even more so after the boys in bed sheets made a house call that late August evening to the new family on Pisgah Ridge.

That was the summer the town spoke of little but the weather:

"Howdy. How ya'll?"

"If I keep sweatin' like 'is, ya'll gonna have to call a lifeguard."

"I tell you what. Can't hardly talk myself into strappin' on underwear."

"Gave it up yesterday myself."

And that was the summer Molly Ann and Molly Ann's brother, Emory, and Molly Ann's brother's best friend Jimbo Riggs, and some spare friends and cousins of theirs all survived the heat by piling into Emory's pickup and heading into the woods. They took with them Molly Ann's mother's castoff Styrofoam cooler they'd pieced back together with electrical tape, and always included in their number Emory's dog, a remarkably chubby golden retriever with a weakness for pork barbecue scraps and Dr. Pepper. In four-wheel drive, they bounced sideways over eroded gashes in the long-abandoned logging trails down to the dark tangle of loblolly pines that hid the Blue Hole.

Whatever drove the adults back in town to raise what they called hell, those fevered, festering troubles, became, at the Blue hole, like Naaman's sores: cooled and healed in the muddy water. At least for a time. At the Blue Hole, white boys from all over Pisgah Ridge and black boys from the valley below swung into daring drops from surrounding sweet gum trees in wild contests of masculine prowess. By midafternoon, when the scent of honeysuckle hung heavy in the air and the heat of the day began to sap the boys' nerve, tight knots of girls with long hair and long lashes and long legs appeared giggling on the banks of the Blue Hole. And the contests resumed.

That was the summer, too, that Molly Ann forgot there were rules and so broke them. She invited the new girl in town to join them at the Blue Hole—less

in a gesture of bold social reform than because it was just too hot to remember about rules.

But Molly Ann Maynard had not thought about that for years, fifteen at least. And she might not have thought about it for years more if it hadn't been for the newspaper and the coffee and a quiet morning alone.

She'd finished her coffee already, the last bitter drop of a pot brewed at dawn, but continued mechanically bringing the mug to her mouth as though she might extend the moment, might trick time into allowing her to stay where she was, unmolested by duties and deadlines. Here, on her brother's enclosed porch, she curled up with *The Washington Post* and basked, warm, content in her corner of sunlight and in that particular swaddling of silence left by the recent departure of young children. She visited her brother's family rarely these days, rarely left Manhattan at all, in fact. But there were times, usually around Christmas, when receiving photographs of a niece and nephew she hardly recognized startled her into making plane reservations. Looking at this year's photo, it had struck her that the kids had lost their baby roundness, looking suddenly so extraordinarily like Emory and her at their ages: fair and ruddy and buck-toothed, little blond gophers.

The children, pulled along by two adults in wool suits and leather shoes, hurry creased across their foreheads, had left for school already this morning. Backpacks and boots and lunch boxes, heroically color coordinated, clattered against the door frame, against the dog's head, against their parents' briefcases. Molly Ann could not have said just how they all got out the door at last.

Mommy, where's my—? Hurry up, please; it's time to—But Daddy she took my—Has anybody seen the—You take my car and I'll take the train, then, if it matters so much that—Just take the green one and forget it—Hurry up, please; it's time to—Well, who cares if Jacob put dents in the side of the green one—But Mommy, she took my—The green lunch box, not the green car—And I mean hurry . . .

But Molly Ann was alone now with the coffee mug and *The Washington Post,* and she was not sorry for it. She turned the page, enjoying the soft crackle of newsprint already unstiffened by two preceding sets of hasty hands.

Molly Ann finally admitted to herself that the coffee mug was indeed empty. She began to put the paper down and prepare for some more productive part of the day, when a photograph on page seven caught her only half-focused attention. A Chevrolet Impala, an older model, parked near the Lincoln Memorial had been flipped, still in its parking spot, upside down, as the picture caption unnecessarily pointed out. Molly Ann turned the paper upside down. She could barely make out a Tennessee license plate, 98-DIXI. *Sequatchie County. . . . Now who'd have guessed you'd remember a thing like that?* she thought. *Forgotten the Spanish explorers and the order of the planets and the difference between red and silver and sugar maples, but still remembered the order of Tennessee counties by population. Shelby County was 1 and Franklin—was it Franklin?—was 2, Knox, 3, and Hamilton, 4. And Sequatchie County was 98.* There was no accounting for memory.

The picture showed a bumper sticker too, though the accompanying article made no mention of it. A Confederate flag on the left half, the right half of the sticker read, "If I'd Known All This, I'd Have

33

Picked My Own Cotton." Molly Ann had not seen that one before.

Someone had apparently set the car on its head in broad daylight, right where it was parked by the Lincoln Memorial—*illegally parked,* the article added meaningfully, as if warning other presumptuous tourists. No one was hurt, and no suspects had been arrested. The incident might never have made the papers had not the Impala's owner insisted upon identifying two black youths found "lurking," he said, "close by beforehand, like they were just waiting." The two youths were residents of, as it turned out, a district halfway house whose director was receiving a prestigious award for community service that very night. The director, the article said, was unreachable by phone.

The Chevy Impala's owner was, however, available for further comment. "You know how sometimes you just have a feeling by looking at people, sizing up a situation. Well that's how it was. . . . But don't get me wrong," he told the *Post* reporter. "I'm not saying all black folks go around flipping good, law-abiding American citizens' cars upside down every day. I'm not saying it's typical of their race, necessarily. I'm just saying . . . well, shoot, all's you got to do is look who's living right down the street there, down past the Capitol, and see how they treat their own property, and if that don't say something about what happens when people go and forget their place . . ."

The award, the article said, would be presented that night as scheduled, though police were holding the two youths from the district juvenile offenders' facility: Hannifa House, it was called.

Molly Ann put the paper aside and closed her eyes. She had once known some Hannifas long ago. Had been friends, even, with one of them—at least for part of a spring and most of one summer. Until a fire one August night; a fire in shapes the Hannifas did not understand but could guess at made the heat of that particular summer just too much, that summer Molly Ann had broken the rules. Didn't mean to, exactly; she simply forgot. That was just the kind of thing the Blue Hole did to you, made you forget about rules.

Growing up, Molly Ann Maynard had few female friends, had always felt more at ease with the roughshod teasing of her brother's friends. She'd been too interested in what she called "big ideas" to join in slumber-party whisperings over boys and haircuts and makeovers—though she tried. There were times she wanted to pack up all her big ideas and consign them to the basement for a single day of fitting in. But she was always awkward and shy and never quite pretty enough to be forgiven those deficiencies. Instead, she carried a certain frustrated intelligence about her like a warning, like a leper's ringing bell: it marred her features, disqualified her slight-built figure from notice.

The new girl in town might have counted as a female friend, except that she didn't count—not as a female like any other, anyway.

The new girl came for just the last week of school. She called herself Shyama Hannifa (which no one, not even the teachers, could pronounce) and said she was from a place called Sri Lanka, which she demonstrated by holding up a flattened right palm to be India with her left fist beside and almost below it to represent the home she said was an island. Her having lived on a real island and her making that map with her hands—not to mention her unpronounceable name—it all made her exotic. . . . Except if you didn't know better she just looked black. So Shyama Hannifa ate her lunch alone in a corner of the sweltering cafeteria and walked alone down the old high school building's concrete-block halls, where the air lay thick and hot, smelling everywhere of locker rooms and chalk dust.

There were no blacks on Pisgah Ridge in those days—the ones who cleaned the houses and mowed the lawns, naturally, but they all lived somewhere else. Various enforcement mechanisms saw to that. Molly Ann could remember learning that lesson early. Once when their mother was driving Molly Ann and her brother home from playing at a cousin's house, they stopped for gas and overheard the boys at Walter's Gas Station discussing current events.

"Heard they hadn't left the house since."

"Smarter'n they look then."

"Always said, learn a stray dog to know you don't want him around, he'll go on back to where he came from."

"J.P. said they's leaving."

"Where to?"

"You care where?" The speaker spit sideways

35

onto the pavement, just missing a paper cup half-full of brown juice.

And the boys at Walter's laughed and one belched and they laughed harder. Her mother, Molly Ann remembered, paid for the gas but didn't buy Cokes there, just to make a point.

But that was a world where the heat—ferocious at midday—and the fumes made mirages of the concrete island, where the tobacco spit sizzled on the asphalt like grease on a griddle, where the Maynards paid for their gas but passed over the Cokes to make a point. That world, the world of Walter's Gas Station, seemed so distant from the one down the logging-camp trails where dark, snarled curtains of raspberry briars opened onto what they called the Blue Hole.

In a way, that's where the trouble began, at the Blue Hole, Molly Ann thought. She sat with her empty coffee cup and her newspaper folded back to page seven with its upside down Impala. Or maybe not at the Blue Hole but because of it, because of what it did.

Later, of course, there was talk that someone should have known better:

"Jimbo Riggs, if you're askin' me. It just didn't look good, and he shoulda known it."

"You lay off on Jimbo Riggs. That boy's as sweet a thing as this town ever hatched."

"Sweet on that colored girl was what he was, if you're askin' me. I tell you what, he was fixing to—"

"Now, now, it's not our place to be layin' blame. But if you was to ask me, I'd say maybe John Maynard shouldn't ought to let his kids run around like a couple of wild Indians. Actin' all surprised when they get theirselves into trouble. . . ."

Most folks admitted the Hannifas themselves weren't really to blame, not knowing anything about Pisgah Ridge, not knowing the rules. The realtor, apparently, had failed to mention how things were.

And Molly Ann Maynard, who knew the rules but forgot, only invited the new girl in town to join them for a swim because she looked so awfully hot looking through her living-room plate-glass window onto big sunburnt patches of lawn.

They'd met a few weeks before at school, briefly, the new girl and Molly Ann, after having nearly collided into one another in front of the water fountain down by the old gym.

Shyama Hannifa had motioned Molly Ann to drink ahead of her. "You may go first."

"No, really, you go ahead."

"I absolutely insist." Shyama bowed just slightly, stepping backward.

Molly Ann drank, then looked up, water still dribbling down her chin. "Cool accent."

"It was the accent you noticed first, was it?" Shyama had asked with a slow smile, something other than a smile playing about the edges of her mouth like shadows on a pond.

"Well . . . your skin's a great color," Molly Ann said then, because it was, though she had to wonder if it didn't sound a little strange, saying it out loud. Shyama Hannifa was the color of cocoa, the kind Molly Ann's mother made from Nestlé's chocolate, powdered sugar, and dried milk, the kind they drank on February evenings when the Maynards played Parcheesi as a family.

"I'm from Sri Lanka," Shyama said, not moving to drink, watching Molly Ann.

Molly Ann knew that, had heard about the map the new girl could make with her hands. She nodded, trying to muster one of the ubiquitous political statistics her father kept about him in scraps of newsprint and shreds of mental notes, more or less properly filed. He was the editor of the town paper and no doubt knew a thing or two about Sri Lanka. He knew a thing or two about everything. Or always sounded like he did anyway, which was the same difference.

Or Molly Ann's mother, had she been there, might have offered something friendly about a second cousin's having visited that part of the world recently—and loved it. Just *loved* it.

"That's interesting" was what Molly Ann managed instead.

"You might know it as Ceylon. If this is India—" Shyama held up her right hand flat against the air— "this—" she placed her left fist by the lower thumb knuckle of her right hand— "this is Sri Lanka." She turned now to drink, lowering from the waist, her back unbent and as straight as though some marionette's string pulled her head upward in one graceful arc. "The accent and the skin are from there," she said.

So several weeks later, from the back of her brother's pickup, Molly Ann Maynard invited Shyama Hannifa to the Blue Hole on a whim. And Shyama had accepted with as little thought. It was far too hot to think clearly.

The Hannifas' house sat on the main road that led off the mountain on its back side. *An ugly house,* Molly Ann thought as they drove by. She saw the new girl staring out the plate-glass window. Molly Ann pounded on the back window of the truck cab.

"Emory, stop! Turn around, Em."

Emory stuck his head out the driver's-side window without pulling over. "How come? You forget the cooler again?"

"No. I just thought I saw the new girl back there in the window. She looked hot."

"You know anybody in town who isn't hot?"

"But that house—you see it? It's horrid. There aren't even any trees. You reckon she'd want to come with us?"

Emory had not formed an opinion one way or another, which argued in favor of his ignoring his sister. But his best friend, Jimbo (James Beauregard) Riggs, who ran the landscaping business with him, said,

"Oh, go ahead. Stop."

"Why?"

"Why not?" Jimbo said and then chuckled at himself because there were plenty of reasons why not, and they both knew it.

It was too hot, Emory decided, to argue with his best friend. So he U-turned back to the Hannifas' house.

Molly Ann poked her head around from the truck bed to the driver's-side window. "Em, you can be real nice when you want."

"Go jump," her brother told her.

The house, a bright red-brick-with-white-mortar affair, was a rectangle, as were the two bare, front plate-glass windows and the pine-veneer door. A little plot of sunburnt, treeless lawn tried to introduce itself as the front yard. No white, Southern pillars softened the home's warehouse front.

Emory's friends in the back of the pickup hushed their swaggering talk and watched silently as Shyama, wearing a long-sleeved cotton blouse and just-pressed shorts, emerged from the red rectangle, heard the offer, nodded, and dipped into the house for her suit.

"You're from . . . ," Emory's best friend, Jimbo, said, pausing as if preparing his tongue for the performance of a new trick, ". . . Sri Lanka." He licked his lips then, satisfied with a good effort. He thought suddenly to offer Shyama a hand as she swung a lean brown leg over the tailgate. But too late. Quick by nature, Shyama's self-consciousness today made her faster, more agile, than usual.

"Sri Lanka, yes. That's right. If this is India . . ." She held up her hands to show them, but stopped, nervous. "You probably know where it is."

"Nobody wears long sleeves here after Easter." That was Josh Hendrix, a second cousin of the Maynards and the youngest of four brothers: Matthew, Mark, Luke—and Josh, a boy who made his father, a Southern gentleman, nervous by saying what he thought when he thought it.

Jimbo Riggs leaned toward the newcomer. "What Josh meant to say was 'How you liking it here?'"

"It's a lovely place, this mountain." Shyama relaxed—ever so slightly. "And how very friendly everyone is!"

Silence followed—uncomfortable, bumpy silence. The back of the pickup seemed to be waiting for her to elaborate. Or maybe just to fill in the potholes of silence with words. "We'd always dreamt about America," she said then, complying. "Dreamt of coming for years."

"*Here?*" L.J. Morton, Emory's closest friend after Jimbo, was incredulous. But then he always had trouble respecting anyone who found his hometown tolerable. He protected himself from the banality of his current existence with a private certainty that he'd been misplaced at birth: conceived not in a gray-slab ranch with avocado green kitchen appliances and orange shag carpet but rather on the city wall of Jerusalem by two vacationing foreign-service agents, unmarried, stationed in Nepal. That he'd been raised in the foothills of rural East Tennessee and not in the heart of the Himalayas, L.J. liked to comfort himself, had only to do with the nature of accidents.

"Here. Anywhere," Shyama answered L.J. "It's all America, my father says, all wonderful." She looked around, unsure of herself. Something, she gathered, was miscalculated in what she'd said.

Josh Hendrix chuckled, evidently at her. "Yeah? 'Bring me your tired, your poor, your naive, huddled masses. . . .' So, what else does your father say?"

Shyama raised her chin on the strength of challenged pride. "'It's the . . . end . . . of the rainbow,' he likes to say," she told Josh, seeming not to like saying so herself. The fabric of her voice was stiffening, bunching into uneven clumps.

Having recovered from the blow of her liking his hometown, L.J. Morton had decided to grant Shyama another chance. She was, after all, someone who had seen the world, seen something beyond this mountain. "Why don't you tell us about your home?" he offered, and sat back for the travelogue.

From the floorboards of the pickup bed where her eyes had been fixed, Shyama's line of vision leveled out with Josh's, then turned to L.J.'s. "This is home now."

L.J. frowned, disappointed. It was a shame. He knew nothing about that part of the world, and he might have included it on his list of Places to Visit Soon, Real Soon. Just as soon as he could break the news to his father, the Lamar of Lamar's Feed and Seed (known in three counties), about the heir to the throne's not sticking around to inherit that millstone, the family business.

But Josh Hendrix leaned forward, across Jimbo Riggs, nearly in Shyama's face. "'End of the rainbow,' your daddy calls it? Anybody tell your family they were coming to the *South?*"

Little Robby Fisher, a baseball teammate of Emory's, piped in with "Pisgah Ridge, Tennessee. Pot of Gold, I always did say."

"Sure," Josh shot back, *"White* Gold."

With his left elbow, Jimbo Riggs pushed Josh's chest back against the pickup's sideboards. "I hope . . . ," he interjected, *"we* hope you like it here." He reached over to pat Shyama's forearm, adding, "Welcome!" then went back to scratching Emory's dog behind the ears.

They rode for a time without chatter, as the knocks and bangs of the pickup riding over the deep-rutted logging trail gradually loosened their joints into friendlier, unguarded slumps, and eventually then, limbered their tongues.

The conversation found a footing on high school sports and high school gossip: a safe terrain of stolen-jockstrap stories and observations, all secondhand, of romances in progress. Shyama's neck and cheeks continued pulsing red—but she began to laugh with the others and relaxed, just barely, her habitually uncompromising spine slouching a little against the rear of the truck cab.

The water at the Blue Hole that first day was empty. Its banks, though, were heavy with teenagers conducting the business of life, their long, lean bodies like big cats, stretching and sleeping and sunning and occasionally striking a particularly gorgeous pose for anyone who cared to admire. Shyama Hannifa, walking last behind Molly Ann and her brother and her brother's friends, stepped from the shade of the loblolly pines to a rock swimming in full sun.

She was dark all right, no mistaking it. Even skin the color of homemade cocoa was dark for this town—too dark to be unnoticed anyway—and made darker still backdropped by deep green. Her hair lay strangely still in the breeze, like uncoiled black licorice on her shoulders.

A glance was exchanged, an eyebrow raised, and then . . . it was finished. It was all right. And so a rule or two got unraveled that day by the ragged hem of the pond.

Maybe it was the steam from the sun on damp rocks that made tight, throbbing teenage bodies wilt into thin strands of quiet, pliant flesh. Maybe it was the nerve-numbing cold of the spring-fed swimming hole that chilled malice into forgetful indifference. Whatever it was, nothing worked here as it usually did. Things didn't get said that might have been said. Things didn't get done that might have been done.

Lethargy or apathy or grace. Molly Ann Maynard never knew which.

All through that summer, while tobacco spit popped and sizzled on the town sidewalks, Shyama Hannifa returned to the Blue Hole with Molly Ann and Molly Ann's brother and Molly Ann's brother's friends and the remarkably chubby golden retriever. And all through that hottest of summers, the Blue Hole kept its tempered peace.

Once, on a Saturday afternoon punctured to near uselessness by thundershowers and drizzle, Emory and Molly Ann stayed home to read and L.J. had to help his daddy in the Feed and Seed and Josh was out camping with his brothers and no one thought to call Robby Fisher, so Jimbo and Shyama went alone. Just the two of them. That time and then one other time.

And even then the Blue Hole, and its peace, endured.

Maybe Shyama never really understood about the Blue Hole, about its being different. Or maybe she never grasped—and this was the truly distressing thing for Molly Ann—that the Blue Hole's being different didn't change the way things were elsewhere.

There was the time she and Molly Ann, after a particularly long swim, lay sunning themselves, rolling their bodies at regular intervals like pork roasting on a spit. And Shyama asked, "Who does . . . Hey, Molly Ann?"

"Mm-hmm?"

"Who does your brother's friend . . . Is your brother's best friend interested in anyone?"

"Who? Jimbo?" An inane thing to say, Molly Ann thought even before she'd finished forming the sounds, given that she had only one brother and her brother had only one best friend. But the question suggested something dangerously amiss.

"Yes. Jimbo."

Shyama's tone sounded casual enough, Molly Ann decided, lying motionless, her eyes closed. Still, it was important that Shyama understand. She had to understand. "Jimbo—you know his momma named him James Beauregard after a Civil War hero, some great-great-great-something or other in the family, which is how she got into the Daughters of the Confederacy, real active member. Jimbo's never been one to go out much. Rather spend an evening reading *Consumer Reports* on fertilizer for the landscaping business and pulling ticks off Emory's dog."

"He's nice looking."

"The dog's a girl."

"No, I . . ."

"Who . . . *Jimbo?*"

"Yes. You don't think so?"

"Why, no. My heavens. No." It was partially true anyway. Jimbo Riggs was not handsome, not really. Dark hair stuck out over his ears in crow's wings because he never could remember to keep it cut. His two front teeth stuck out slightly too and just barely crossed; his nose was a little too large; his eyebrows, a bit too bushy. Still, Jimbo Riggs was one of those creatures who is cute—irresistible even—for no particular reason. Jimbo Riggs himself rarely spoke, but his green eyes did, always looking like he was up to interesting mischief. And his dimples (without the full consent of their owner) said flattering things women wanted to hear. Even a best friend's little sister could see the attraction, though Molly Ann chose not to say so just then. "I don't know that Jimbo's your type."

Shyama propped herself up on one elbow. Molly Ann could feel her staring. But Shyama said no more of Jimbo Riggs that day, and never brought it up again. So maybe she did understand about the Blue Hole. And what was not the Blue Hole.

Still, Molly Ann thought now, wading back through years of memory, a bit murky now, still it must have been baffling to Shyama—to the whole Hannifa family—when the boys in bed sheets came to visit that night. The truth was, what happened in late August took all of them by surprise, even the ones who might have remembered to think how things were.

They'd left the Blue Hole later than usual that particular night. Emory's pickup, with Molly Ann and Shyama and Emory's friends aboard, stopped at Hog Wild, a sawdust-floor establishment some called a restaurant, others called a joint. Run by Levi Steinberger and his daughters, the place served pork barbecue, hickory-smoked for at least two days, and equal to none in the county. Levi Steinberger, who never ate the stuff himself, kept the recipe locked tight within the family circle—and with it, made himself a valued community member the local Commerce Club could no longer afford to exclude.

So Molly Ann and Emory and Shyama and Jimbo Riggs and L.J. Morton and Josh Hendrix (little Robby Fisher might or might not have been there, nobody could ever remember) wiggled their bare toes in sawdust as they talked, lingering over pork barbecue, cold Cokes, corn on the cob, and Dr. Pepper that Emory's dog drank straight from the can. By the time they stopped by the Dairy Queen for chocolate-dipped cones, the fireflies were damping their lights for darkness to put the town to sleep. They sat in the grass enjoying their cones, enjoying each other's company, enjoying the easy quiet of a summer evening—until Shyama said she should be getting home.

When Emory's pickup pulled into the Hannifas' driveway, three other trucks were already there—just leaving, in fact. Their wheels spit gravel and dust, turning the hot, humid night air into a kind of suspended paste. Molly Ann and Shyama and Molly

Ann's brother's friends and the just-wakened golden retriever sat in the back of the pickup without speaking. Without moving even. Except for Jimbo's reaching to hold Shyama's hand. Molly Ann choked on the dust, then continued, like the others, to stare in silence.

They all recognized the trucks; no need to say so.

Molly Ann Maynard had seen the pointed white hoods and the gowns once before: last summer when the Klan set up a road block and stuck deer rifles in driver's-side windows and collected cash in Kentucky Fried Chicken buckets because no one in town thought to tell them they couldn't.

But they'd looked, she thought at the time, like children at Halloween playing ghosts with their mothers' best sheets. They held their rifles cradled, like nursing infants, and the eyeholes of their hoods didn't line up real straight with their eyes. So you had to wonder how much trouble they could actually cause.

This time, though, one of them had at least managed to see out straight enough to light a match.

The fire that consumed, and partially exploded, the Hannifas' only car had by now nearly burned itself out at the head of the gravel drive. Only a steel frame still smoldered.

But another fire, this one on the Hannifas' lawn, writhed, a frenzied dance reflected in savage orange triangles: jagged remains of the plate-glass window. Even now, Molly Ann could recall the smell of that smoke, heady and sweet, that poured from two perpendicular pieces of blazing wood. Like some maimed beauty, some crude inversion of good, the burning cross washed the Hannifas' front yard in garish orange light. Screaming sickly, wearily as it fell, its left arm and then its right collapsed onto the lawn as they watched.

"Better call the fire department," Emory had said at last.

"They were just here," Molly Ann said. Josh Hendrix nodded. And no one ran to the phone.

Inside the house, they'd found buckets and pans enough to douse the flame. Mr. Hannifa had the rest of the family inside kneeling before the living-room window. Back and forth he rocked, holding to his chest the stone that had shattered the window and his evening peace.

Mr. Hannifa had meant to leave his religion behind him when he got to the end of the rainbow—had announced as much to his family and friends. But tonight he faced east. Bowed. And prayed. While Molly Ann stood wondering what to do. Molly Ann's mother, had she been there, would have asked in her third-grade-Sunday-school-teacher tone, "Now what would Jesus do?" She was maddening that way. *Jesus,* Molly Ann thought, *would face east, kneel, and pray along with the man.* But Molly Ann wasn't Jesus, and she just stood there, feeling stupid and ashamed and in the way.

Shyama stood by the silver cobweb of shattered window with her back to the overpopulated living room. Her posture stiff, unmoving, she remained there past the dying of the last embers, when the scorched earth disappeared beneath night's black upholstery.

Josh Hendrix and L.J. Morton stayed to help sweep up shattered glass, then walked on home. Jimbo Riggs left the Hannifas' last, just behind Molly Ann and Emory. And only then did Shyama turn to say goodbye, her spine stiff, her handshake quick and hard, with a feel of such finality in her touch that Jimbo Riggs kicked with his toe at glass on the floor and said, "I'll write."

The Hannifas' heeded their first warning, despite the pleas of a few of the more liberal town members, John Maynard, newspaper editor, for one, who wanted someone—someone else—to stand up to the Klan. But the Hannifas didn't need to be instructed in the history of Reconstruction to understand that a car blown up in their driveway and a cross burning in their front yard and a rock heaved dead center through their living-room window constituted a clear warning. The Hannifas were moving North. "Just *North,*" Shyama told Molly Ann. But failed to leave an address. And Molly Ann had failed to ask. So that was it. That was all. They'd come to the end of the rainbow—and found it on fire.

As it turned out, they all went their separate ways not too long after that anyway. Jimbo Riggs took over Lamar's Feed and Seed when Lamar Morton suffered a stroke. (Lamar's son, L.J., was working at the time for the Peace Corps in Togo—or was it Tonga?—Molly Ann never could remember which.) The Feed and Seed worked well alongside the landscaping business. After he bought out Emory's half, Jimbo renamed the business they'd begun as boys.

Big Dog Lawn and Garden Beautifiers he called it now, after his best friend's retriever. The big dog herself, overindulged to the end, had breathed her last in the shade of an old dogwood tree where she was supervising the spreading of cedar mulch. She was buried with an unopened box of barbecue scraps and a Dr. Pepper, memorial gifts from Levi Steinberger and daughters.

Little Robby Fisher left town to play professional baseball. No one heard from him, and no one particularly noticed. Josh Hendrix became a defense attorney in Birmingham, Alabama—and sometimes, it was rumored, waived the fees of certain black clients. Back home his father still grieved the son's lack of diplomacy and tact.

And I, Molly Ann Maynard thought to herself, *I became dazzlingly successful as a consultant in Manhattan. And after years of cultivating big city sophistication, still prefer Emory's pickup to my Saab, Steinberger's barbecue to Legal's Seafood lobster, and male friendships to female—though who has time for either?* Molly Ann's marriage, to a man equally successful as she, foundered in the first year.

Jimbo Riggs, Molly Ann recalled now, never married, which seemed a waste. He always was such a sweet guy. His mother was said to be inconsolable over the fact that her boy had never found anyone—now that she'd recovered from the scare years ago that he might have done so—some dark-skinned little thing whose name nobody could pronounce.

Molly Ann lifted the coffee mug to her mouth again, surprised once more to find it empty. She set it down by the phone and picked up the receiver, dialing 411, then the number of the halfway house the operator had given her.

"I was wondering," Molly Ann began, "that is, I read about Hannifa House—or the mention of it, at least—in the *Post* today, and it's silly of me, really, but I thought just maybe . . . is there, by any chance, a *Ms.* Hannifa there?"

"She's in a meeting right now," a secretary's voice said, smooth and well oiled. "May I have her—?"

"Well, yes. Really? I—actually, no, I just wondered if she . . . if this . . . Is this a . . . By any chance might this happen to be a Ms. *Shyama* Hannifa?"

"That is our director's name. Who may I say called Ms. Hannifa?"

"Called. *Really?* Because, you see, it was just a guess, a lucky shot. Called. Yes. That is, better yet, are there . . . I was wondering, might there be any tickets still available, maybe . . . , to the banquet?"

"Tonight's banquet?"

"Well, yes. Actually."

"I'm afraid not. Not for some time. But I would be happy to relay a message to—"

"Could you tell your director then . . . Let's see . . . Could you tell her it's a friend from Tennessee who'd like to join you tonight? From Pisgah Ridge, tell her. Forgive me. But could you tell . . . ask her that? Please."

"I'm sorry," the secretary said, having checked again, her exasperation seeping out now between the cracks in her professional restraint. "The invitations have all gone out. Thank you for call—"

"Wait. I apologize. But could you—" Molly Ann paused, stumbling for a moment over her own audacity. "I'm sorry, but could you, could you tell . . . could you ask your director, could you check to see if she . . . remembers a place we called the Blue Hole? . . ."

The Marriott banquet hall was like every other of its kind—luxurious in plush mauves and emerald greens and crystal chandeliers—completely predictable, which was part of its appeal. Molly Ann Maynard entered with a bevy of guests in black ties and cocktail dresses who milled around, carefully, conspicuously, using one another's names, bandying about yet-bigger names, and laughing a great deal. Above the speaker's podium hung a great vinyl banner that read, "Celebrating the Hannifa House: A Safe Place, a Good Place, It's Your Place."

Caucasian faces, the minority present, swam eerily pale in the browning wave of guests. Molly Ann wondered which of the guests were Hannifa House residents, which were sincere supporters, and which were clever politicos who sensed the perfect opportunity to appear compassionate in public.

The tables teemed with young faces, some of them already hard-edged, chiseled out of something other than merely childhood matured. These were interspersed with middle-aged faces, some prematurely wrinkled by golf-course tans and a little indiscretion or two. There were older faces too, some quiet, noble, at peace with their years, others pinched between seasons of professional ambition and personal compromise.

Molly Ann watched a boy of no more than thirteen, his hands drawn up in tight curls to his wrists, hobble in to a table dragging a side-turned foot. Two youngsters in wheelchairs raced for places at the other end of the room, taking one waiter and a busboy with them, quite involuntarily, as they went. A young woman just taking her seat had chosen fishnet stockings to wear with a skirt quite short and heels quite high, disrupting in her wake a conversation or two. Two men and a woman Molly Ann recognized as senators, though she couldn't recall their names, sauntered by with drinks in hand.

Molly Ann could not make out what all the people she saw before her might have had in common. Nothing, she supposed, except the Hannifa House. Whatever that was.

She thought of *The Washington Post* and the Chevy Impala upended and wondered if in fact the deed had been done by Hannifa House boys. And she found herself hoping it had.

The room temperature was climbing. Some computerized thermostat had gone haywire, sending a managerial-type Marriott employee staggering about, sweat-pimpled and red in the face, earnestly attempting to solve the problem.

Molly Ann watched as black ties and black dresses floated table to table, the corporate world, the political world, the world of the street, those who sold their bodies and those who sold their souls and those who sold others' bodies and souls, the compassionate and the corrupt, the blameless and the blatantly self-seeking, all mixing in that moment according to some strange inexplicable formula that seemed to have no bearing on profession or race or age.

Intoxication or heat exhaustion or grace, Molly Ann Maynard couldn't have said which, but the Marriott banquet room sat simmering in loud, overdressed, but unmistakable good will.

Molly Ann moved then from her place just inside the doorway, running smack into an entering guest, surely one of the very last, so full was the room by then. "Pardon me," Molly Ann mumbled, recovering, just barely, the balance of her own high heels.

"Please," said the woman. "After you."

"No, really, you go ahead. I—"

"I absolutely insist," said the woman. Molly Ann Maynard thought for a moment the woman was holding up one hand for her to stop, then realized she'd flattened the palm of her right hand and lifted the left in a balled fist beside, nearly below it.

"If this is India . . . ," began Molly Ann Maynard, and the woman, who was laughing, held out her hand.

Please Repeat after Me
These Outrageous Words

There is in any marriage ceremony that moment when time snaps to attention and life pauses in its fidgeting. The very rafters strain to hear two people clasp hands and offer to sign the blank check of the vast unknowable years ahead. Before they have uttered a word, a bride and a groom announce in carefully choreographed steps that they are trusting the balance of their lives, their riches and their diseases, their achievements and their accidents, to the care of another.

They have lived, these two, not even a third of their lives, maybe not a quarter, yet they parade past long pews of soundlessly cheering crowds towards promises they have understood only well enough to say yes to—but not well enough to understand what living that yes means: a thousand seemingly insignificant decisions that, when totaled, either sustain or bankrupt a partnership.

In the moment of the marriage vows, long white train tangling in the wake of hope, little else matters: the gladiolas never opened as the florist said they would, so the bridesmaids must march down the aisle cradling great big asparagus stalks; the best man put the bride's ring in the toe of his shoe for safekeeping but forgot to transfer it before the ceremony to a more accessible place; the flower girl, whose dress is more elaborate than the bride's, refuses to budge from her seat at the back; wedding attendants lock their knees and keel over in the hot June afternoon like privates in a military parade; the groom's parents boycott their son's day in continued protest over his not marrying another Korean. . . . In the end, though, the laser focus of the exchange of vows burns away all else but two people being asked to make pledges, an utterly outrageous set of promises, before God and these witnesses.

Over the past seven years as a part-time minister, I have performed an ever shifting conglomeration of tasks: some I loathe, some I bungle, and of some I count myself extraordinarily fortunate to be a part. Officiating in marriage ceremonies falls into this latter category—at least in the cases of couples I know well, know their faithful intentions, and can think confidently of their future together. The real privilege of the task comes when two people look each other in the eye and say not, "Just let me check my calendar—and your bank balance; I'll see if I can't work you in" but rather, very simply, in two lean, long-underrated words, "I will."

Time and time and time again, when that moment comes to say "Repeat after me," I am agog that two people of generally sound mind are willing to do so. And I wonder if they are hearing all those big, big, big little words lobbed to them: forsaking all others . . . , be faithful *only* to . . . , with this ring I promise to *always* . . . I pray at those moments—passionately, fervently—I pray that they're listening closely to themselves.

Do they know? Do they understand? I wonder. There can be midnight places in a marriage from which they may not be able to see the daybreak return of peace—much less ecstasy—out ahead. And sometimes holding on in the dark can feel like more than anyone should be asked to do.

Yet, those outrageous words . . .

My husband and I both work in Cambridge, Massachusetts, a university town. Because our community of friends and parishioners is, predictably, ever transient and ever young, my husband and I are often on the road. We perform marriage ceremonies in state parks and mountain chapels and the occasional stately church sanctuary, wherever the Cambridge diaspora has landed this time. We work as a team. ("A husband and wife," some wedding guests say, "marrying a husband and wife, how symbolic, how strange, lovely, touching, odd," as though we were a traveling circus act.)

To stand before two painfully eager faces, to watch trembling lips sound out words that hang there sparkling in the silence, promising passion and friendship and loyalty, is to share in a moment of the most sacred intimacy. It is also a sober reminder to us. No matter what ferocious disagreements we may have had over the content of the wedding homily—or, more likely, over a tone of voice used when discussing the content of the homily—we, too, stand still and wonder again at those impossible words: *for worse, for poorer, in sickness, to cherish, till death* . . .

Love as I love, quivers on the crest of that moment. *Love her, love him, as I love. And this is love.* . . . With flowing headpiece and earnestly brushed hair and brimming eyes, the bride and the groom look at you. They swallow hard, and they try to speak. They strain to respond on cue, their breath snagging on awe (the men, I've long noted, often are more overcome with emotion in the moment—maybe because they did not expect to be).

You've counseled them, cautioned them, encouraged them in private. Yet here in public, in the presence of their friends and their families, you wonder if they understand, really get it. Maybe there was something more you should have said—about the sacrifice. And the gift . . .

To have and to hold from this day forward . . .

I often wish I had a videotape of a late-October morning more than seven years ago: Boston City Hospital. The phone call came from a friend saying that her husband, father of their four young girls, had been hit by two cars, drag racing. He was riding his bike home from work. For the first time in probably a thousand rides, he had not worn his helmet.

For better, for worse . . .

It looked bad.

The accident shattered vertebrae that could slice into his spinal chord at the base of his neck. His lower jaw was loosed from his upper, and his upper from the rest of his face.

He looked bad.

Paul had landed on his face. His nose, for all practical purposes, no longer existed. His cheekbones stabbed upward, making ripe plums of his eyes. His mustache was peeled from his upper lip and dangled irrelevantly from one side of his face—what had been his face. He was unrecognizable.

For richer, for poorer, in sickness and in health . . .

When my husband and I arrived at the intensive care unit, Paul's wife, Jan, was in the waiting room, standing there—*still able to stand!* I thought at the time—with a strength that sets some of us apart in crisis. She suggested we go straight in to see Paul. If he knew we were there that day, or any of the other days in the merciless weeks that followed, he gave no sign. We did not stay in intensive care long that morning. Couldn't.

We did sit with Jan a long while, going over the stray-cat details that do not go away just because the walls—the whole world—comes tumbling down. Someone still had to pick up the kids from school; one of the girls had a birthday that next weekend; the insurance might or might not sufficiently cover all bills; someone still had to . . . so that Jan could be with Paul, regardless of whether or not he knew she was there.

To love and to cherish . . .

After hearing the medical explanation (from a surgeon using a plastic skull to provide visual demonstrations for the oldest daughter) of what had become of her husband, Jan stepped back through the swinging double doors into intensive care.

"I held his hand," she said simply when she returned. "And I told him—" she glanced away only once, briefly, to blink off tears—"that he was sexy."

Till death do us part.

Surgeons of all sorts pieced Paul back together little by little, and therapists retrained his physical and cognitive functions so that no outward signs remain of his accident. I never would have believed it possible.

For any couple contemplating marriage, I often wish I could hold up a picture of Paul on that late-October morning at Boston City Hospital. I wish I could place Jan's I-told-him-that-he-was-sexy as a caption underneath. I'd like to say to the couples that unless they are ready to accept that kind of ugly glitch in their dreams, unless they are willing to look tragedy in the face and hold its hand, then they'd better not take another step forward—invitations in the mail or not.

I'd like them to know too that there are also simple, daily choices in a marriage potentially as destructive as a disfiguring physical accident. And unless they are willing, these two, to sometimes dwell in dark, ugly places for a time, unless they are willing to learn the painfully acquired skill of climbing back out together, unless that is the courage and the tenacity and the grace they have brought with them here today, then they had better back up and keep quiet from here on out.

But for those who have read the fine print and understand it and are still willing to sign, for those who have the wisdom and the capacity for wonder, the compassion and the guts—and also the joy—for those and only those: Please repeat after me these outrageous words. . . .

Better Than Seven—
or Close

There is in Jewish and Christian Scripture a touching story about a woman and her daughter-in-law—or about a woman and her mother-in-law, depending on your perspective. The story, sandwiched amongst long lists of laws and family lineage, lies in the mercifully succinct book of Ruth. For anyone learning to translate Hebrew, it's a good beginners' slope; and for anyone learning to translate their own communication style to that of their in-laws, it's good for a chuckle.

Naomi, whose name means "pleasant," is a widow, the mother of two sons (now dead), and the mother-in-law of two women who have failed to give her grandmother status. For all these things, she is only just bitter enough to threaten to change her name to Mara, which means just that. Bitter. There's self-expression for you.

But she retains something of a sense of humor. When her daughters-in-law try to accompany her back to her homeland, she lets them off the hook with a liberating bit of sarcasm, demanding to know if they're waiting around to marry the second batch of sons she's not yet borne. One of the young women seems relieved, understandably, to be given an out. She returns to her own people. But the other, Ruth, insists on staying with Naomi.

Ruth's response to her mother-in-law is recorded in a Scripture passage frequently read, ironically, in wedding services as a commitment between husband and wife. But "May the Lord deal with me, be it ever so severely, if anything but death separates you and me" (NIV) is actually a pact between two women. In fact, in the entire story, which includes the account of Ruth's deftly securing a new husband for herself (and a financial provider for Naomi), the only mention of "love" appears in the final chapter, when several other women observe the extraordinary devotion of Ruth—who is "better than seven sons"—to her mother-in-law.

Amazing. A lovely story.

Lovely. But not mine.

I am not of the better-than-seven-sons class of daughters-in-law. I wonder how many of us are. Consider the following announcement made to a woman with twice your wisdom and experience (we won't mention age): you plan to carve out your own substantial share of the affections of the son this woman bore after thirty-two hours' hard labor ending in a C-section needlepointed together by a palsied intern. Welcome news? I think not. Still, I've often wondered if some women don't come equipped with more in-law-friendly features than I do.

Like Ruth, I am a sort of foreigner among my husband's family. But unlike Ruth, I travel to their homeland only on round-trip tickets. And even living three thousand miles away on an opposite coast, I still somehow stick out among them: the East Coast square peg, a lobster-trap ornament on a Los Angeles lawn.

I am the reticent newcomer agape and wide-eyed in the rough-and-tumble affection, the high-volume hilarity, the abundant advice-for-life from a numberless (to me) family of Southern Californian Italians (extroversion upon extroversion). I am the blue-eyed, dishwater blonde floating like toxic waste in a glossy sea of dark eyes and darker hair: swift and certain disruption of the gene pool. "The Tall Swede," one cousin calls me. In stiletto heels, which I do not wear, I'm 5', 5'3/4" tops. The family's Big Auntie Angie reaches my nose and can't possibly weigh enough to give blood.

In marrying me, my husband set adrift an inept—let's be honest, *dangerous*—cook into an ocean of enigmatic lasagna recipes—recipes demanding ingredients suspiciously unattainable at 7-Eleven. Early in my married life, I once attempted a culinary obstacle course in my husband's family's heirloom recipe collection, *Man Pleasers* (a woman in pinafore apron on the cover). In the process, a hanging wooden shelf containing a dozen cookbooks (wedding gifts all) fell on my nose. All twelve books *plus* shelving: directly on my nose. This sign from the kitchen gods I took to heart. I now enter their domain only to make iced tea—in the microwave.

Once, just once after that, I did attempt to tackle one of my own mother's culinary specialties, cornbread with sour cream, from a recipe printed in a Southern church cookbook. When the cookbook caught fire, I quit. We keep it—its remains—handy on a top shelf in the kitchen as a kind of visual aid for anyone who cares to ask who does most of the cooking in our family and why.

Somehow, I think Ruth, in my shoes, could have pulled off a mean lasagna for Naomi and family. Or cannoli with a properly crisp pastry shell. But me? I do the laundry. Happily.

Then there is my inexplicable lack of passion (even indifference) towards food. Though slim to a person, my in-laws remain at all times within the three-count spin of the Italian-family culinary waltz: anticipation of future food, analysis of current food, and reminiscence of past food consumption. Participants may be called upon at any time to recall emotionally charged details of meals eaten a decade earlier. Calabria never produced my type: a big fan of Velveeta cheese and sweet pink wine with the screw-on top.

Now, I've never had trouble *respecting* my in-laws, my mother-in-law in particular. I admire the steeliness of a woman who successfully raised two boys single-handedly; the recklessness of a woman who parasails but cannot swim; the selflessness of a woman who, regardless of the lack of personal financial padding, always finds someone else's nest to feather first. And from the first, I was in awe—okay, fear—of a woman who cleans the extremities of her kitchen floor with a toothbrush.

From the beginning, I marveled at her.

We just seemed, early on, to have so little in common. I grew up in the east Tennessee foothills, south of Soddy Daisy, and until I was twenty-four, thought Chattanooga was a big city. She was born in East

L.A. and insists her idea of nature is two different kinds of sidewalk. When my mother-in-law visits us in New England, she is plucky, cheerful even, shivering under four layers of borrowed winter wear: a size-5 woman turned matreshka doll. But she is clearly baffled at our choice of climatic zone. I, on the other hand, take a kind of perverse pride in the residual April snow in my backyard—and I regard with real suspicion those who pick grapefruit out of theirs.

Compared to her home's sleek contemporary decor (impeccably clean, of course), our nineteenth-century farmhouse, with its wide plank floors (with spaces in between just right for sweeping dirt into), yard sale antiques, and eighty-seven-pound lap-dog wanna-be, appears very nearly unfit for human habitation.

My mother-in-law sends baby gifts to her late husband's great-uncle's grandson. My sense of family intimacy is not so acute. In my most recent long-distance chat with my brother in Washington, D.C., I learned that his wife is four months pregnant with their second child and they've put their house on the market. The wife is the same one, though.

Being clumsy with the Family Thing, I do not often manage to translate fond thoughts into tangible expressions of devotion (a forte of my mother-in-law). I could not, for example, compose an on-the-spot speech as touching as Ruth's to Naomi. And living three thousand miles away from my mother-in-law probably disqualifies me from borrowing Ruth's version. But I think of her often. (Often, too, I'll recall a recent crack of hers and laugh aloud—typically in some very inappropriate setting.)

On her most recent Boston visit with us, it hit me that something new is happening. In the past, my mother-in-law waited hand-and-foot on her boys, hovering over the skillet while they ate. Now, as her son made tempura, slaving over a sputtering fryer, I watched her, alongside her daughter-by-marriage, learning the unspeakable pleasures of sampling another's food, another's work. In that moment, that soft-stepping pirouette of time, life quietly reversed itself. The servant was served.

Uneasy and guilt-ridden at first, she relaxed with commendable grace into an uncharacteristic posture of ease. Not that she'll stay there indefinitely. She'll bound out to defend the rights of immigrant workers or scratch mildew (invisible to the naked eye) off her bathroom tile or buy baby gifts for the newest son of a third cousin twice removed. But as her son dished out the second course for her dining pleasure and mine, I watched her slide cautiously into this new other role, as if accustoming one toe at a time to a scalding-hot bubble bath. She's in now. Bubbles to her neck.

I think she likes it. I think she may even like me. Not seven sons' worth, maybe. Still . . . this could be the beginning of a beautiful friendship.

Sandy Springs

She'd arrived early, not quite knowing why. Maybe she wanted to breathe in the smell of the gym without people actually in it, before the band (assuming they'd hired one) began tuning up, before bodies filled the hollow echo of empty bleachers, vast wooden canyons. Beneath backboards too silent and nets too still just now, the hardwood of the polished floor gleamed. It smelled of wax and rubber—and slightly, too, of human perspiration. It smelled like a gym, like *this* gym had always—should always—smell. And maybe that's what she was looking for. Something familiar, but not recently so. Something connected to a past that, if shallow, was happy in its way, heedless of anything but the careless wending of its own course.

Grief crashed over her in a wave then, crushing the little courage that had gotten her here, making her feel again the fragility of her life right now. There were days, and this was one, when she impressed—and surprised—herself merely by remaining on two feet, by not collapsing under the sheer weight of tears dammed up behind the superficial pleasantries and the mundane business exchanges of everyday life.

That she'd arrived early was strange, she confessed to herself. That she'd come at all, stranger still. Daniel would have had plenty to say about this evening. He'd have enjoyed himself. Not because he would have fit in, but because somewhere along the way he had learned to enjoy watching other people's discomfort at his not fitting in: watching them fidget, pinched between the dual realities of what they expected and who he was. He'd have reveled in being the only black man here—and the only Asian. He'd have stared each person in the face and smiled winningly and waited, just staring, while those who could muster up some semblance of courtesy tried to figure out what sort of foreigner little Chrissi Mitchell had gone and married.

"How *do* you do?" he'd have asked, upper and lower teeth touching, in the accent of the overly educated New England classes. "Charming town you have here. Perfectly charming. Chris has told me so much about all of you and this fine, *fine* establishment, her old high school. A delightful place, this. Truly delightful." Chris had watched him operate over the years. People liked Daniel because they could not help themselves, because Daniel left no possibility for anything else. He might intimidate some and bewilder some, but people, all sorts of people, liked Daniel. Even Stanley P. Green, assuming he showed up, would have liked Daniel. Though the two of them would have had absolutely, unquestionably, nothing in common—except having been in love with the same woman.

Daniel, of course, would have made an archaeological dig of the evening, would have rolled up his sleeves and relished this night. He'd have wandered about, his professorial horn-rim glasses pushed far up on his nose, enthusiastically inspecting fossils of his wife's early history.

Chris backed away from the center of the floor where the big blue letters of "Sandy Springs High" still needed painting. She wasn't as comfortable there as she'd once been. Maybe it was the pom-poms that had given that extra confidence—a kind of I-belong, I-count, I-matter feel in their broad plastic handles and the brazen swish of blue-and-white paper hair. But adults, she'd found, couldn't wander about with blue-and-white pom-poms dangling significantly from their briefcases, perched saucily upon their Power-Books.

There at the center of the floor, she and eight others had once lined up two to three nights a week. They had executed well-practiced bodily contortions with variations on the bend of the leg, the flex of the foot, the point of the toe. So much depended upon the set of the leg, the foot, the toe. Sometimes late at night to make Daniel laugh, she'd resurrected old cheers from the farthest outposts of her memory and performed them with all her early wide-eyed earnestness in the center of their Cambridge, Massachusetts, apartment.

Ro-o-ock ste-e-eady . . . , she'd shouted at half volume and moved at half-speed, out of deference to the Italian landlords downstairs. They had commented once—at least once—upon these rituals: "Chri-i-i-si, the bumps, the bumps, the bumps; you wake-a the dead."

Daniel never tired of it. "And on these skills, ladies and gentlemen," he would say after a particularly compelling performance, with a low bow to the invisible audience in their living room, "was built a future."

"And a glorious future it is, too," Chris would say, acknowledging her public. "Today, my dear friends, you see before you a woman whose extraordinary talents and early training got her where she is today: wallet stolen, tires slashed, life threatened. And that was before lunch. Thank you. Thank you. No applause is necessary, really." She and Daniel would collapse on the secondhand sofa laughing—at themselves, at her, at her past.

The past she'd gone looking for now. Wanted just to brush up against, again.

Chrissi Mitchell found a bleacher seat that suited her. Front row, way in the corner, over by the door, the door her school team burst through after halftime pep talks, spirits recharged to a voltage their high school bodies could not sustain into the fourth quarter.

Chris listened to the gym and could hear distant— far distant—squeaks and roars and, at the center of the sound, hollow thuds, slow and rhythmic, steady as a metronome. Suddenly its beats came in rapid succession accompanied by the screech of rubber treads and human skin on polished wood. Rubber slammed against metal and young bodies against one another. Then the satisfying swish of rubber brushing nylon, the net's fibers stretched with the triumph of an instant. They might win. They might lose. Better yet, they might be injured—and Sandy Springs High would drape itself in fondling, cooing concern over twisted ankles and wrenched quadriceps and displaced kneecaps.

Stanley P. Green, Chris remembered, had often

been among the injured, the pampered.

"What's the score, Chrissi?" she thought she heard someone call.

"We lost," Chris answered out loud before realizing she was still alone.

Dodie Whitmire was the first—the first of people on time, that is—to arrive, looking just as she had fifteen years before. Maybe a few pounds slimmer. She'd always carried around in flesh a full extraperson more than her bone structure seemed to appreciate. And she'd worn thick-lensed glasses that changed shade according to available light, which effectively hid her one good feature. Her hairstyle was unaltered: still pulled back from her face into a kind of collapsing bun impaled by silver bobby pins. *What she lacked in real beauty freed her to be smart,* Chris thought now. Dodie had excelled in everything academic available at an underfunded public school, and she won her fellow students' respect by being the kind of person they knew instinctively they might have to work for one day. She was voted class secretary not because she was popular but because she was competent. And because the class president, Marty Weathersby, a second-string fullback revered for the quantity of beer and women he could consume at parties, would clearly need someone else in charge.

Right behind Dodie came Kenny Hughes and Melody—what was her last name?—but they'd gotten married right out of high school, so it didn't really matter anyway. Four children trailed behind them, gift-wrapped in bow ties and pink sashes. They were here on time only by accident, having mistaken the party's starting time. Typically, they arrived everywhere late or not at all, the children acting as dragging anchors on an overloaded merchant ship.

At least Stanley P. Green had not arrived yet. Chris was not at all sure she was ready to come face to face with that particular part of her past.

Chris raised herself from her corner of the bleachers and took a deep breath. Time to reminisce, to recover musty old memories. Time to flip through faded photographs of the lithe young bodies that yearbook captions insisted once belonged to someone present tonight in the gym. Time to exchange fifteen years of history with people who once exchanged daily litanies of last night's phone calls. Chris moved forward slowly, reluctant to give up her current advantage of seeing without being seen. But the front row of the bleachers, even on the opposite end of the gym, was not much of a hiding place once Melody and Kenny were through checking their children for chocolate smudges and Dodie Whitmire looked up from a notebook no doubt detailing the evening's agenda. Dodie would be good at that.

"Hello, Dodie," Chris said, still several feet away. "Anything I can help with?"

Dodie looked up from her notebook, her glasses sliding down the bridge of her nose as she did so. She nudged them back up with one shoulder. "Well, I'll be darned. Chrissi Mitchell. We didn't think you, of all people, would be here after Debbie Jo told us . . . I'm terribly sorry, Chrissi."

"It's been awhile now. Over a year. I don't do very well keeping in touch with folks here. Sorry I never sent back the reunion letter. Didn't know I'd be here myself."

"Glad you are. What are—" Dodie glanced toward the main doors, where bodies had begun to meander in. The Hugheses had been joined now by several other couples and a whole boatload of children, Chris observed.

Did there have to be so many children? She hadn't thought about children somehow when she'd pictured herself making it through this night successfully. Every night for over a year, from a too-large double bed in Cambridge, she had fought the stark facts of the present, had been kept from sleep by the din of a too-silent night. Then, just recently, she'd envisioned herself reaching back for the past and finding something there to help her make it through the wasteland she feared ahead. But children—she hadn't counted on that.

"I'm sorry, Chrissi," said Dodie. "Will you excuse me? My job's only just begun. Can we talk later? So glad you're here." Dodie gave Chris a quick hug and trotted away to disperse nametags.

Chris and Daniel had meant to have children before too long. They'd meant to have a few more years, just the two of them, snickering over nachos like college kids late at night with David Letterman; hoarding frequent-traveler miles on unstable, desperately generous airlines to spend a week in Ankara or Galway or Asunción; howling over one of Daniel's Philosophy of Religion class papers ("As we see in the parable of the Protocol Son . . ."); holding each other all night after the funeral of another one of Chris's boys. Shooting victims mostly. The occasional stabbing. Never an overdose. They were all too poor for an overdose.

Someone squeaked. *Like a field mouse with an East Tennessee tremolo,* Chris thought, recognizing the sound as distinctly feminine, distinctly Southern. "Why, Chrissi Mitchell. Is it still Mitchell? Did you ever get married, sugar, or did you just string old Stanley P. Green along all these years?"

Coming towards her was Dawn Marie Majors—*Brandy.* She'd changed her name in junior high when she'd dyed her hair platinum, learned to paint with cobalt blue eyeliner, and landed the head-majorette position.

"Hello, Brandy. How are you?"

Brandy squealed again. Chris tried to remember if there was a switch to shut her off. "Chrissi Mitchell, don't you how-are-you me! Girlfriend, get over here and give me a hug."

Chris did so, aware of a hulking masculine form providing the backdrop. "Nice to see you, Brandy. Is this your—?" Chris stopped, plumbing her brain for some forgotten fact of Dawn Marie Majors's

marital history. What had Debbie Jo told her?

"My fiancé," Brandy said, her back to a creature clearly overdeveloped in the pectoral region, a breed nearly extinct in Cambridge, Massachusetts. Brandy was mouthing in exaggerated word pantomimes something Chris couldn't quite make out. Hadn't there been a husband before this, right out of high school? Maybe one after that as well.

"Congratulations. I'm Chris Mitchell."

"Ronny Gold."

"Ronny's with the Steelers," Brandy dribbled.

Chris smiled and tried to guess what Daniel might have said—assuming he recognized the Steelers as a professional football team. It was still early in their dating history when she discovered Daniel had never been to a football game.

"No," she'd said. "No way. I don't believe you. How could anyone—let alone a boy—grow up in America not having been to see a football game? It's not possible. Like never having had a hotdog with mustard and ketchup and relish spilled in your lap! What's an American childhood without football games and relish stains?" It frightened her that any healthy, red-blooded American male might rather spend Friday nights studying German through correspondence course because his rural Massachusetts high school didn't offer it.

Daniel had been amused, and unrepentant. "And how is it that you, Ms. Mitchell, grew up not only in America but in the Bible belt and never have gone to church?"

"But that's different, of course. That was a matter of belief."

"Or lack thereof."

"Or lack thereof. Have it your way. But a way of rebelling against the norm, at least."

"And football would be . . .?"

"So I shunned religion. But we're talking about *football* here." The next day she had bought them tickets to the Harvard–Yale game. Afterward, Daniel declared it an enjoyable afternoon since, as he and his students liked to say, Harvard won, 28-28.

Daniel's mother—who'd begged coaches to leave her 6'2"-in-ninth-grade boy alone—was Korean. His father, who traveled most weekends preaching revivals, African-American. Late at night in their Cambridge apartment, to make her laugh, Daniel would imitate the gospel choirs of his boyhood. He sang at the full volume of a rich-textured baritone, improvising the appropriate gestures and claps and swayings to gospel adaptations of old hymns: . . . *the solid Rock, Rock, Rock I sta-a-a-and; All other ground, ground, ground is sinking sand; All other ground is sinking s-a-a-and.* But he never would imitate his father. That was sacred territory. And he would not allow her to say he was making fun of the choirs, only imitating them for her benefit. It was all holy ground. She learned to tread there shoes off.

"What position do you play?" Chris remembered to ask Ronny Gold.

"Tight end," Brandy answered. Letting her do the talking, Chris thought, seemed a mutually satisfactory policy. Ronny Gold looked in danger of running out of vocabulary if pressed. "And I'm manager of the Marshall's lingerie department over at Southgate." As she spoke, Brandy gazed up at Ronny Gold and hung a bit of her weight on his hand, a sturdy hook. "And just what are you doing with yourself these days, Chrissi?"

"I work with juvenile offenders. Boys. In inner-city Boston."

"Oh. My. Heavenly days."

"I do it for the money," Chris added, for no particular reason. "Excuse me. Real good to see you both. Nice meeting you, Ronny."

Chrissi Mitchell staggered around tight knots of conversations and whirlpools of hugging, swirling arms, and laughter, everywhere, laughter: the heightened pitch of manufactured hilarity.

"Chris, you're here." It was Debbie Jo. Debbie Jo without any little ones in tow. "I got a baby sitter," she said before Chris could ask. "Thought the little gumdrops might feel in the way while Mama saunters down Memory Lane. Lord knows they'd been in the way, whether they'd felt it or not, the precious angels. Bill's gonna stop by later. Not much into this kind of thing; you know him. How you holdin' up, hon?"

Chris fell onto her friend's shoulder, alarmed for a moment that the tears might come now, unheeded, might wash her clear off her feet, might thunder over her reserve and long-practiced poise. Might leave her looking like the blasted pile of rubble she felt. Debbie Jo gripped her shoulder. "Steady, girl. C'mon now."

Chris inhaled deeply and gradually raised her head. "What's the deal," she asked finally, not caring particularly, but needing to hear Debbie Jo's voice, "with old Brandywine?"

"This one's esposo numero tres, last I counted. The woman's a regular retriever. Just keep throwin' good-lookin' men down her path, and she'll keep goin' after 'em. You seen Stanley P. yet?"

"No."

"He's here. Somewhere. Saw him a minute ago, askin' after you."

"Did you tell him?"

"I just told him to take a number, that everybody wanted to see Chrissi Mitchell come back home to Sandy Springs where she got her big start."

"Big start. Big start to what? I went out to change the world and got hurt crossing the street."

"Now stop that. You've done things with your life, built it on things that mattered. And, you know what else?"

"Hmm?"

"That shade of blue is just real stunning on you: does that help?"

"That helps."

The night moved on in a haze, sidewalk-chalk

figures in the rain. Soft, muffled voices asked polite or pointed or stupid questions made mandatory by a chasm of fifteen years. The band—a low-budget, long-haired, short-breathed affair—sawed out creaky renditions of old Eagles and Little River Band and Jimmy Buffet hits.

"I'd liked to of seen him . . . that is, *met* him," one old friend, suddenly flustered, told Chris. "Heard your husband was a real smart fellow. Real unusual type. Where'd ya'll meet, anyway?"

They'd met when she worked the morning shift at the Graduate School of Arts and Sciences cafeteria. Punched in at 5:30 and by 6:00 the line opened—with no one in it but the die-hard scholar types. Daniel was usually first in line, his Hebrew flash cards or Teilhard de Chardin or James Cone stacked precisely on his tray beside the bagel (habitually lifted from a long line of better-looking pastries) and low-fat cream cheese. To that, he added the one large coffee she poured him every morning. She burned herself at least once each morning because her eyes—not to be trusted to remain open for another half hour at least—kept closing during the process.

"You should really get more sleep," he'd say every morning. "Really you should."

"Thank you. And you," she'd say, leaning across the counter and smiling groggily into his face, "should mind your own business."

One morning he asked if she'd like to do coffee sometime. "I gave you yours," she answered, burning her hand with a meandering ladle of milk gravy that missed its target biscuit, missed the entire plate. She opened her eyes to see what was scorching her hand and noticed then he was nice looking. Most definitely nice looking. She'd never dated a black guy before. And only one Asian—her father would have had a fit if he'd known *that*—curl right up and die.

So it started with coffee. By the time things took a turn for the more permanent, her father had his say and spent the next several years sulking—which was better than Chris had hoped for. Daniel's father had embraced her with a warmth tempered only by concerns over what Daniel liked to call her Existentialist Agnosticism with Smile on Face. "Sartre," Daniel teased, "would not recognize his own insights, so cheerily rendered."

And years of knowing Daniel and his family had changed all that anyway, had partially pried up the bolted-down pieces of carefully crafted skepticism.

Chris wandered amongst the clumps of people, often accompanied by Debbie Jo's watching, maternal eye. Chris heard old friends' recent histories, looked at photos. In strings of innocuous vagaries, she responded politely to cherished pictures of their beloved strangers.

Darryl Dennis—who'd been, was it Student Council president?—had a new sales job. "Takes me away from my family a lot, but the pay's real good, and I mean *real* good, so what can you do?" He had a picture of his new home, a whopper of a structure with the predictably magnificent in-ground pool. "And in a *good* neighborhood this time. You know our last one took a sudden turn for the worst—no offense, but you know what I mean."

Charlie Putman and J. D. Doyle brought their families to every Friday-night Sandy Springs home game, and their sons were playing football—full pads, even—in elementary school. And you could already tell they'd be better than their old men, they

said, which—they were pleased to hear—everyone agreed was impossible.

Missy Mohler (stage name Holly Sierra) couldn't make it to the reunion on account of prior professional engagements. But she sent along a recent biographical sketch and an 8″ x 10″ glossy via Cindy Hicks, who always meant to make it big too (having starred in senior year's *South Pacific),* but along the way forgot about needing to leave town someday.

Delia Sprague, who'd played first clarinet in the band, served Chris a Coke.

"You still living close by, Delia?" Chris asked her.

"Not anymore. We moved clear down by White Oak. How 'bout you? Nobody's seen you in forever and a day."

"White Oak, is that . . . ?"

"New subdivision down to the lake, 'bout fifteen minutes up the road. Where is it you're living now? Somebody said you got married but not to anybody from around here."

Chris handed Delia the ice tongs she'd dropped. "Moved even farther up the road. New England."

"Geez. Cold White North."

"Hmm? Oh. Right. Spring comes a little later than

some folks might like."

"You know Stanley P. was looking for you, Chrissi? Ya'll ever talk anymore? Was I ever shocked to hear ya'll broke up!"

"Not so much anymore. Talk, I mean. Fifteen years maybe."

"Thought sure ya'll'd end up together."

"Guess we'd been together for a while back then. It's good to see you. Thanks for the Coke, Delia."

Michelle Sandersen, who practiced corporate law in Atlanta, had brought her new husband, who practiced corporate law in Atlanta. The two of them stood aloof, urbane, and bored. "And what do you do now, Chrissi?" Michelle wanted to know. "Someone said you'd gone to graduate school. Glad to know someone in Sandy Springs left town besides me."

"I work with gangs. Drug dealers. Pushers. Pimps. Only the worst of the worst, I like to think. La crud de la crud. In Roxbury. Up in Boston."

Michelle raised one eyebrow in a face still stiff-creased with the effort of appearing interested. "How terribly noble of you. And what is it you do with your . . . clients?"

"Gang treaties, some days. Literacy, others. Most of the time just pray they don't make lace of each other with their little toy guns. Those aren't the good days."

Michelle raised one more eyebrow. "Can't say I'd have pictured you . . . doing what you're doing." She swiveled a perfectly smooth pageboy in her husband's direction. "Chrissi was one of our peppy, popular types. Stanley P. Green's girl. Little Miss Sandy Springs Everything."

"Most Likely to Succeed," Chris helped her out. "Kind of peculiar, isn't it? And look at me now. Life's funny that way, don't you think? Pardon me, won't you, while I slip over for a drink. Nice seeing you all." But she didn't quite make it back to Delia Sprague at the drink table.

"Why, Chrissi Mitchell! Chrissi!" Kenny and Melody Hughes flagged her down to meet their children. Aside from a slight difference in height, Chris found the four chubby bisque-faced beings indistinguishable. A scrubbed and polished matching set.

"Our lives just *revolve* around them, you understand," Melody said. "Children just take over your life. They *become* your life. But you must . . . Do you have children, Chrissi? Where's your husband?

We'd heard you were married up North—to some—to someone up North," Melody said.

Chris pulled a snapshot from her wallet, tilting it their way without releasing it. "Daniel Washington. My husband. He died last year. Jogged every day, ate right. Never would share my french fries. Died of a heart attack. He was thirty-eight."

The Hugheses stared at her for a moment before they managed to take in the picture. "Awful sorry for you, Chrissi," Kenny said.

"We are that," Melody said. "Sorrier than sorry. And maybe," she added a bit tentatively, "maybe the Lord was protecting you, your not having had any babies yet." Kenny nodded. Chris looked from one to the other, wondering exactly what they meant: knowing exactly what they meant.

Chris heard again her mother's sobbing when she and Daniel had announced their engagement: "And what about the children? The poor, poor children? Has anybody thought about the children?"

"Nice to see you," Chris told the Hugheses at last. "Good to meet the kids. Lovely children." She turned to look for Debbie Jo but found someone else standing there, waiting his turn to talk with her.

Stanley P. Green (Stanley R. was his father) was taller than he'd been in high school, tanned, more muscular than when he'd been the high school running back. Overall better looking, Chris thought. She'd hoped in some strange way he wouldn't be.

"Well. Hi ya, Stan."

"What's this, no hug?"

She hugged him from the side. And then, because she did not want to, she made herself take a step back. "So you're . . . still sailing?"

"You look terrific, Chrissi."

"Thanks. Same to you."

"Wish I could say the same for everybody here. The merchant marine's been a great place for me."

"I'm glad to hear it. Really glad. Then you're not sorry you lost those years by switching over?"

"Not for one day have I been sorry."

"That's nice, Stan. Where is it you're living now?"

"Just bought a condo in Bermuda, already had a home in Key Biscayne. I'm getting married."

"Well . . . that's great. I wish you many . . .—" the fault in her voice trembled, widened— "happy years together."

"We met last spring in Australia. Ashley's a dancer

there." He yawned. "She has a kid, by someone else. Don't care much for the kid, but he comes with the deal. Somebody said you married some black dude."

"Worse than that," she told him. "An intellectual."

"Ho! Worse and worse!"

"The smartest and the kindest and the most intriguing man I've ever known."

"Now, now, you'd hate to say *ever*. Why's he not here? Not as smart as you think if he trusts his wife here alone with an old boyfriend she dumped in a moment of mental instability." He grinned at her and winked.

Somehow, she couldn't tell Stan Green about Daniel just then. It was taking all her energy to keep back the tears. She reached for Stan's hand, squeezed it, and turned away.

Catching her elbow, he glimpsed enough of her face to change his mind about what he'd planned to say then. "Chrissi . . ."

She turned back slightly but kept her face averted.

"I was really hurt, you know. By you."

"I know. Me, too. I'm sorry. I always figured there were plenty of women in line to help console you."

"Didn't say I was lonely. Nothing women love more than a man with a broken heart. Did you ever miss me?"

She reached up to pat his shoulder, felt all too well its sculpture, and withdrew her hand. "Just that one shoulder," she said. "That's all I missed." They watched each other's eyes.

"No regrets, Chrissi?"

She looked away, then back, and shook her head. "No. No regrets."

She turned away again.

"Wait . . . Chrissi, before you go, I . . . just wanted to wish you . . . fair winds and following seas."

She smiled, at least tried. "Merchant marines?"

"Merchant marines."

"Thanks, Stan."

"And Chrissi?"

"Hmm?"

"Ashley won't call me Stanley P. either."

"I think I'd like her." She squeezed his hand again and walked away, quickly this time, leaving him to learn from someone else why little Chrissi Mitchell's husband, who didn't come from around here, hadn't accompanied her to the class reunion.

Chrissi Mitchell felt free to leave then: to leave the cotton-stuffing air of the gym, the faltering, flat beat of the band, the faint mildew of memories too long preserved. She was finished here now. She might not have enjoyed herself as much as Daniel would have, had he been there to return all the stares with his big, charm-the-lint-off-your-stockings smile, his horn rims sliding up and down his nose as he laughed. But she'd come and she'd survived. That was enough. She slipped out the gym's rear door to the parking lot beside the football field, sat down heavily on the brick wall leading to the football locker rooms—and wept.

Debbie Jo's face appeared at the door of the gym. "You want botherin' or not?"

"Only if it's only you."

"Only me. You wanna tell me why on earth you came in the first place?"

"Haven't the foggiest. Just seemed like things were simpler or easier, like there was less to hurt over when we were all back here together. Strange idea, I know."

"You always were one for strange ideas, Chrissi Mitchell." Debbie Jo hugged her, stroked her hair.

They sat for a while in silence, a silence the length and depth of which the friendship of their younger years never tolerated, always felt compelled to fill in with chatter. Now, they embraced it, together with each other. "Have they been monsters?" Debbie Jo asked at last.

"No. Some. Could've been worse."

"Your Daniel would've made big fans of them all. I never saw anything quite like him."

"Been thinking the same thing all night. Hey, Deb?"

"Yeah?"

"You ever wonder why your life turns out one way and someone else's another?"

"Sure."

"Tonight I came feeling scared—maybe a little sorry for myself."

"Uh-huh. 'Course you did, hon. Anybody would in your shoes."

"But I don't feel sorry about the past anymore. Just sad about things now—but not sorry. It's important, that difference. I'd have wanted to make the same decisions again. That's why I had to come, see?"

"No." They sat again in silence. "But that's okay. As long as you see."

"I'd do it over again. Even knowing what I do now, I'd still have ended it with Stan and moved North and bet everything I had on a good man with bad heart problems and a bunch of street kids with . . . heart problems too, I guess. I'd do it again."

"'Course you would, hon. Though why, just to figure that out, you had to fly a thousand miles to come drink flat Coke with people who don't know they haven't got what it takes to wear Lycra anymore is beyond me."

"It's just . . . maybe it's not a bad thing to come back home and find it isn't home anymore."

"And that helps?"

"That helps."

"Then I'm glad, hon."

"Hey, Debbie Jo?"

"Mm-hmm?"

"You know this song?" Chris stood up on the brick wall and with all the appropriate gestures and claps and swayings, she performed Daniel's gospel rendition of an old hymn, specially adapted for their Cambridge, Massachusetts, apartment: . . . *I sta-a-a-and. All other ground, ground, ground is sinking sand. All other ground is sinking sa-a-a-and."*

"You're a strange one, Chrissi Mitchell. Stranger than ever. Which helps me know you're gonna be okay. C'mon back in with me. I need another drink—or three—before I pick up my kids."

Womb Without End. Amen. Amen.

I was not—am not—one of those admirable women who glow (what *does* that mean anyway?) when they are pregnant, who have in their eyes a look of secret rapture, who will tell you straight-faced that they have never felt better in their lives. Such women are not to be trusted.

Though I did not glow when I was pregnant, I will admit something in my face must have announced the change long before the rest of my body made it so *abundantly* clear. The day I told a dear chum of mine that I was expecting, she handed me a book on pregnancy she'd ordered weeks before.

Just had a feeling, she said: a certain look about me. (Indigestion perhaps.) Within the next months other gifts followed. One was a bottom sheet for a crib. Since both my husband and I had to ask why there was no top sheet, it was clear to everyone we were two people needing instruction in expecting a baby—and whatever was to befall us after that. My friend's book was invaluable.

But the author's tone frightened me. The list of possible discomforts she told me to expect went something like this: fatigue, constipation, skin blotches, abdominal pain, backaches, leg cramps, increased urination, incontinence, shortness of breath, flatulence, bloating, heartburn, indigestion, faintness, gum irritation and bleeding, hemorrhoids, varicose veins, nasal congestion, nose bleeds, nausea and vomiting, increased heart rate, and swelling of the hands, feet, and face. Oh, and stretch marks. Eager for the Complete Pregnancy Experience, my body made sure I missed out on none of the above. But that wasn't what scared me. It was the women the author kept quoting—with a tone of hearty approval. Page after page after page they insisted that pregnancy was the highlight of their lives.

These are not women I want to meet.

I spent forty weeks (telling women "nine months," as it turns out, is just a public-relations ploy to assure propagation of the human race), *forty weeks* trying hard to be cheerful. I was cheerful at four in the morning riding the exercise bike for backache troubles. I was cheerful at four in the afternoon responding to the candid observations of total strangers on the vastness of my waistline. And because pregnancy is such a happy public spectacle, total strangers were cheerful with me when the enormity of my own personal space caused me to misjudge theirs—and to topple small children and protruding mailboxes in the process.

I was even cheerful at my thirty-nine-week milestone when one of my most cherished (to that point) colleagues and confidantes demanded I join her for a Red Sox game. Ninety-five-degree heat. Bleacher seats in full sun. Surrounded by skinny, leggy high school girls in short shorts and midriffs.

And I might even have managed to be cheerful when the guy on our row who got up each inning for beer repeatedly complimented what *must* be, he said, one *whopper* of a baby I was carting around. Having apparently confused me with the Buddha, he seemed also to need to pat my tummy on each pass—for good luck, I supposed. I tried glowering and scowling and turning away and *not* turning away (just try squeezing past a sideways pregnant woman in Fenway Park bleacher seats), but he, thoroughly drunk by then, was far too cheerful *not* to pat my belly. I finally thought I was going to have to beat him up. I was by this point, after all, the bigger of the two of us.

Yet, even as my whopper of a baby (okay, so he was right) made use of nine innings by treating my bladder like a trampoline, still I made pleasant comments about the weather and the pitching.

To myself, though, and to my husband and a few close friends (who, if they thought me a whiner, had the grace not to say so at the time), I admitted that I resented bearing all the discomfort of pregnancy while my husband—compassionate, understanding, eager to help though he was—stayed slender and annoyingly, from all outward appearances, unaffected. No quantity of foot massages, fabulous cooking, and cleaning the cat-litter box could make me call it even.

Why do women have to be the ones? I wanted to know. Why is it always the *woman* whose professional deadlines must wait if pregnancy puts her to sleep by seven each night? Why is this *our* child, but *my* varicose veins?

I once asked my sister-in-law, soon after the birth of her first child, if she resented the fact that her husband, my brother, never had to suffer through the pains of childbirth. (She'd already, to the horror of my mother, an only onetime grandmother at that point, admitted the pain to be excruciating.) My sister-in-law looked at me from some distant place I could see in her face but not touch. "I felt . . . sorry for him—sorry he couldn't be as much a part . . . ,"

she said, exchanging coded smiles with my mother. And in that gentle tug, the tacit alliance of that moment, the two women stepped towards each other across a generation of differences, leaving me alone and incredulous.

I wonder if I have since told them both that they were right. Not that they need to hear me say it to know they were. Or to know that I understand now, understand why the two of them looked, that day, bound together—to each other and to the invisible host they represented: the countless millennia of women who have been overburdened and unspeakably blessed with the privilege of bearing life.

A close friend of mine had her first child three weeks ago. By the time the attendants let my husband and me in to see her, she was already chuckling (a bit weakly, granted) over her own behavior under recent duress. She'd had one of those labors that zooms from zero to sixty leaving the possibility of having an epidural back with the rubber on the road. During the final stages, she repeatedly yelled through her pain at the nurse, "You have *no idea!* You have *no idea!*" The nurse, it turns out, had three children herself. She calmly retorted that she did, in fact, have a very clear idea: so shut up and *keep pushing*.

My sister-in-law and my mother and my mother-in-law and plenty of friends tried to explain it to me beforehand. I suppose I wasn't paying attention. Or maybe I just cynically ignored it all as hype: products of maternal instincts I did not possess.

So childbirth, the bloody wonder, the messy, magnificent spectacle of it, took me by surprise: the power housed in pain, the joy poised and waiting as a head and a shoulder and another shoulder and two legs—count them: two!—come struggling into a struggling world. For an instant there amidst blood and water, torn flesh and new life, celebrations begun before the suffering is over, we see the face of God.

I know that not all births are planned or desired. And, yes, I know too that not all births are joyous occasions, that there are those who must grope their way through the tears to pack away their streamers, their cigars, their plans.

Friends of my parents had a daughter who was expecting the very week of my own due date. She delivered a baby, their first, the same time as our baby. That much I knew. But after my labor was over, my parents told me the rest of her story. The baby was born dead, the umbilical cord wrapped around its neck.

I don't know that mother's name, where she lives, anything about her—except that the doctors suggested she spend time rocking her baby before they buried it. Rocking it and grieving for it and getting used to the idea that it would never know her face.

I don't know that other baby's mother, but I sat and rocked my child and cried for the young woman who was rocking hers before she would have to bury it. And I prayed, though I've no idea what I prayed. Maybe sometimes tears are a prayer.

So I am that much more ashamed now, saddened too, that for forty weeks (not nine months), I had to *work* at being cheerful. I carried a child who had been planned, who was wanted, for whom there would be food enough and toys too much and even a room of her own.

Few of us stand, on any given day, equipped for tragedy. Few of us are ready for grief so profound we can no longer even feel our way into the wet, gray haze of the future.

I have learned, though, that few of us are any better braced for magnificence. In the average course of the average day, few of us are really prepared for the wonder left strewn behind mystery, shimmering on the wake of a miracle.

So childbirth took me by surprise.

I have learned that there is sometimes wonder waiting—even for the unprepared.

I have learned that there are moments in human existence in which worship burns in our very bones, in which our spirits tremble and our reason quakes as we glimpse the molten center of life. For new body draws new breath the moment pain gives way to power. The two shall become one and one shall become two and strength is made perfect in weakness: I tell you a mystery. We have grasped the hand of God this day and found language insufficient, save one word only: *Yes*.

Peanut Butter on Fine China, French Wine in a Paper Cup

Now as they went on their way, Jesus entered a certain village, where a woman named Martha welcomed him into her home. She had a sister named Mary, who sat at the Lord's feet and listened to what he was saying. But Martha was distracted by her many tasks; so she came to him and asked, "Lord, do you not care that my sister has left me to do all the work by myself? Tell her then to help me." But the Lord answered her, "Martha, Martha, you are worried and distracted by many things; there is need of only one thing. Mary has chosen the better part, which will not be taken away from her."—Gospel of Luke

Any thoroughly modern woman would applaud the story of Jesus at the home of Mary and Martha: the good teacher shakes his head at Martha (poor frustrated, frazzled soul, who fervently believes the bundt cake's popping out of its mold *in one piece* really matters on some universal scale) and then proceeds to praise her sister, Mary (who prefers theological discussions to playing the perfect hostess).

I appreciate what the story says about Jesus and what it says about the way women's minds should

85

(and should not) be occupied. Still, something about the story makes me shift in my seat and check my agenda and . . . thank heaven Jesus isn't coming for dinner tonight.

Now personally, I've never feared that Jesus would say to me what he said to Martha. Among my volumes of sins will *not* be listed spending too much time with the Cuisinart when I could have been listening to Jesus. My husband and I believe in egalitarian marriage, and because he insists on indulging in dishes outside the realm of my own specialties (Pop-Tarts, Cheez-its, granola bars), he performs the culinary feats in our house. But what worries me—genuinely so—is that I'm not at all sure Jesus would commend me for being like Mary, either.

Here's the thing: Jesus makes me nervous. God Almighty, Omniscient, *Mysterium Tremendum,* is one thing. But Jesus makes me uncomfortable. (Though as far as I can tell, Jesus made everyone uncomfortable—which is reassuring at least, to not be the first to fidget and fuss at the idea of him.) Imagine asking the guy home for dinner. Not only does he not lend a hand in setting the table or pouring the drinks, he's got your other would-be helpers spellbound, sitting at his feet imbibing the profundity of the ages while the pot roast withers and the salad wilts.

And how on earth does one prepare for Jesus' dropping by? Would you clean the house more thoroughly than usual?—Or, let's be honest, would you clean the house *for a change?* Or would excessive cleanliness suggest that you'd let spiritual advancement opportunities go loping by? Would you borrow fine china to celebrate the momentous occasion, to show your deep and abiding respect for Holiness—or use paper plates to symbolize an equally deep and abiding lack of interest in material goods?

Would you impress him more with a Maine lobster menu, the edible version of pouring perfume on his feet? (He did, after all, apparently know *quality:* in perfume, in wine, in widows' mites, in human hearts. . . .) Or would you fare better slapping peanut butter and jelly on day-old bakery bread, using the money you saved to buy groceries for the single mom with five kids down the street?

Slippery business, this.

You can imagine Jesus praising either. Or condemning either. Accompanied either by "Good and

Faithful Servant" or "You Whitewashed Sepulcher," depending, of course, on nasty little intangibles like motivation and intent.

It's that lack of ordinary predictability that makes me nervous. Well-mannered people smile and mumble polite vagaries when a faux pas catches them entering the mop closets of other people's private lives. Jesus, on the other hand, strides in quite intentionally past all the tell-tale clutter of buckets and rags, broken promises, and dry-rotted dreams. And before so much as setting his backpack down, Jesus would be asking a guest how her fifth husband—or was he just a live-in?—is proceeding with the delinquent child-support payments to his former wife.

To invite Jesus over for an evening would be to entertain trouble: the kind of guest who would welcome the neighborhood rabble trying to crash your best party. The kind of guest who would let trespassers pour dubious-smelling foreign substances on his feet—and all over your floor. The kind of guest you'd be glad to leash to the barbecue grill and leave there awhile.

The Gospel accounts agree on this much: Jesus called 'em like he saw 'em. And public opinion swayed him no more than storm-stirred winds and waves. A desirable trait for a Little League umpire. But a regrettable lack of tact in a dinner guest.

Faced with the predicament of hosting him for supper myself, I think I'd serve peanut butter sandwiches on fine china with French wine in paper cups. And if I could muster up the courage, maybe I'd tell him the truth: sometimes he makes me nervous. And sometimes I'm not sure, not specifically blueprint sure, which are the things to be done and which left undone. And then it might occur to me to apologize to him for not inviting everyone to dinner who might've wanted to come.

And then the group of us would sit down, on the floor, I think (assuming I'd remembered to sweep in the recent past). And the dog would come deposit her eighty-seven pounds beside him, no doubt, and anoint his bare feet with her fond canine drool. And maybe he'd smile. And while he scratched her behind the ears and pulled off a tick or two, he'd teach us, once more, what God's love is like.

And I'd listen. *Listen.* And wish I knew whether to wipe his now-slimy feet with my hair or whether to say something philosophically astute, intellectually dazzling. . . . And no doubt he'd probably point to the nearest child and suggest I learn about God from her.

Maybe then I'd just sit and listen. Eat peanut butter sandwiches off fine china and drink French wine from a paper cup. And take what comfort I could in the fact that somewhere tangled deep in my discomfort was a heart willing . . . to be made nervous.

What the Gardener Knew

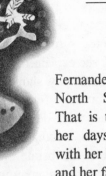

Fernande Pierre was a North Shore gardener. That is to say, spending her days on her knees with her back bent double and her face nearly touching the earth while the wind off the sea burned her lips a chapped, scorched brown, that was what she called her work. Her husband, Jean Paul Pierre, called it playing in the dirt. She'd borne him eight children (two of them breech) back in Haiti and kept all of them alive on plantains and rice and tomato paste that might have sufficed for two—but ten. . . . Still, they endured—precisely because Jean Paul Pierre's wife did not play. She merely believed in spending as much time on her knees as it took to survive.

It was through the barometric warnings of this woman's wide-set eyes that Jean Paul learned to gauge her emotions. Reflected in those tarnished brass surfaces was never desperation or fear. Particularly not fear. Fury—now that was another thing. Sometimes, late in the evening as they scraped off layer by layer of their work clothes (careful to dirty only a portion of the clean floor), Jean Paul might mention, say, the year 1991, a bad year—worse than usual for Haiti—just so he could watch his wife's eyes spit sparks. The darker skin that ringed her eyes would twitch and jump. The muscles of her shoulders enlarged and knotted, she would swing their hulk towards him like a lioness turning on her kill.

Fernande Pierre, who did not play, had once worked as a maid in Boston, in a four-story brownstone on Beacon Hill. The house was owned by a friend of a friend of the mayor, all of whom believed in the strength of the private sector and in cutting government benefits to the poor, in eliminating them entirely to undocumented workers. But the friend of the friend of the mayor always hired one or two unlikelies for his own personal service: his own contribution to charity. He believed in charity.

Fernande Pierre, the maid, worked out well, for a while. But then the Beacon Hill brownstone closed up for the spring and summer while the household moved to conduct business at the Cape during those precious, too-fleeting months of warmth and sun, long walks by the sea. Fernande suggested she work as gardener instead. But the Beacon Hill brownstone had no garden to speak of, only a cobblestone street in front of the imposing brass and lacquered-oak front entrance. And a diminutive brick courtyard in back with a few potted impatiens, which the friend of the friend of the mayor sometimes remembered to water himself. So the owner of the brownstone recommended Fernande Pierre, with caveats, of course, to an old friend of his—a former wife, in fact—who preferred the refinement and expanse of her North Shore home to the cramped, vertical elegance of Beacon Hill.

Fernande Pierre could understand Madeline Bradford's attachment to the old North Shore place, or so Fernande's face said for her during the interview. Madeline Bradford liked the privacy, she said, created by a big house surrounded by acreage and the sea. And besides, she explained, her great-grandfather had built the place. Why shouldn't she live there, even if it was a bit large for one?

Calmly, impassively, Fernande Pierre looked around the grounds, nodding, asking one or two questions in a quiet, deliberate French. She seemed not at all surprised, this woman with eight children and a husband just from Port-au-Prince who couldn't yet find work, that a middle-aged woman might choose to occupy seven bedrooms by herself. Maybe it was for this that Madeline Bradford liked her.

Fernande Pierre had not asked how the grapes growing along the veranda's arbor that faced the sea were disposed of. Nor had she challenged orders to coddle the ivy—because it looked so very *established*—that climbed up the three stories of whitewashed brick (though it did tend to pull out the mortar over the years and peel black paint off the shutters). She had said nothing—and appropriately so, Madeline Bradford thought—when told of the horrors of too many, too hungry squirrels invading the property, some of whom annually got themselves trapped in one of the six chimneys and either starved or were burned to death: each spring their skeletons had to be cleaned out by the sweep. Fernande Pierre apparently understood that such a horde of uninvited scavengers could not be tolerated upon these private grounds, or so her unflinching demeanor said for her. And so she was hired.

It also didn't hurt that Fernande Pierre made Madeline Bradford feel smarter, more sophisticated than usual even, when the gardener spoke to her employer in a slow, carefully enunciated French. (Haitian Creole she saved for the living, growing things in the ground.) Madeline Bradford, wondering if she herself might not be fluent in two languages after all and never have realized it, spoke to her gardener in English only because the proper French verb tenses would never quite come to mind, though remnants of prep-school vocabulary remained intact. And Madeline Bradford felt clever, too, because she'd

clearly hired for herself what proved to be a dedicated worker, quite apart from what neighbors had warned her regarding the work habits of Haitians.

Arriving a good hour early each morning in a '74 Ford LTD, Fernande Pierre obediently parked down behind the gardener's shed, where the car could not be seen by guests. She typically had her tools out and ready in time for her to sit—for only a moment—to watch the sun turn the northern Atlantic sea from black to rose to steely blue. Fernande Pierre enjoyed her work, or so said her face, at least. Left alone most of the day now that she had her instructions, given in English and carried out in silence, she spent long hours nearly prostrate, squeezing and crumbling the cool earth, only recently thawed. Her long days were spent stroking and pruning and poking at the brittle skeletons of trees and shrubs and vines that Madeline Bradford couldn't even recall having owned. To the gray, rotten shroud of New England winter's remains, Fernande Pierre spoke: days on her knees, her back bent double, her face nearly touching the earth. And from its cold frame, Fernande Pierre seemed herself to cause to rise the red tulips and grape hyacinths that lay in broad bands among great islands of daffodils.

In late May, Fernande Pierre was even seen to smile once or twice at the lilacs' abundance: lavender tumbled mound upon mound at the veranda steps, which opened out to a stone walk leading down to the sea. And by June, all along the path the pink rhododendron and the deep scarlet and white azaleas praised her labors, said in soft drifts of delicate beauty that Fernande Pierre had properly translated the directions on the packages of fertilizers, had caught just enough of the rattled-off old-timer's tips from the man at the nursery, had made just enough friends among the North Shore Riding Academy's stable hands—and had not come entirely empty-headed from her homeland.

In mid-June, Fernande Pierre began a perennial garden of her own devising, in a shady bare spot where the sloping lawn met the slick, blackened boulders of the beach. Using transplants from the already overcrowded flower beds at the front of the house, the gardener arranged lamb's ear and bleeding heart and cyclamen and astilbe and bluebells, backed and bordered by hosta and cinnamon fern and hydrangeas. All in the shape of a large kidney. She'd

seen similar gardens at Madeline Bradford's neighbors'. But Fernande Pierre's lilies grew more lush; Fernande Pierre's lilacs bloomed longer; Fernande Pierre's roses climbed higher than those of the North Shore neighbors. On her knees, her back bent double, her face nearly touching the earth, Fernande Pierre burrowed her fingers in the dirt, felt for moisture and for drainage, inspected the most remote branches for pests, pampered the new growth through the sudden near-killing cool of New England spring evenings.

Madeline Bradford noticed all this before her neighbors did. That is, she noticed not what the gardener was doing so much as how this spring and this summer, as never before, color and strength and grace trembled in the breeze off the water. In comparison, the plantings of her neighbors looked like overplanned, expensive little tracts from a hurried nursery man's catalog: unremarkable, unimaginative little plots, utterly interchangeable one with another. At length, even Madeline Bradford's neighbors had to admit she'd made a clever choice of gardener this time, and dropped by to inquire the gardener's secrets.

"Je suis désolé," the gardener would say with a

sad shake of her head. *"Je ne cherche que ce qu'il faut chercher."* So those who could not understand her French, who attributed their not having ascertained the secret to simply a language barrier, went away better satisfied than those who could understand her words, but not her. They were left to stomp back up the stone steps to the big white house muttering, "'Only look for what needs looking for.' Indeed. Cagey, tight-lipped devil."

Madeline Bradford loved to entertain, enjoyed filling her big house with summer Sunday-brunch guests floating by like so many sailboats, their white linen dresses and navy sport coats flapping in the sea breeze. But this summer, Madeline knew, would be particularly successful, having, as she did, the most stunning grounds on this stretch of the North Shore. Such magnificence was worthy of admiration. Madeline purchased a half dozen more Adirondack chairs, painted white, and had Fernande Pierre strategically arrange them with views of the ocean framed by views of roses and hyacinths and lilacs and rhododendron.

On Sundays, Fernande Pierre stayed home with her family. Madeline Bradford allowed for this ab-sence with good humor, even though the centerpieces suffered from a lack of fresh cuttings from the gardens. One Sunday, though, Madeline was forced to insist upon the gardener's presence—just this once, she explained. Important people, deep blue-blood specimens from Boston Brahmin families associated with the symphony and the Museum of Fine Arts, with publishing and politics, would be present for brunch. A more than usually lavish menu had been planned. Having Fernande Pierre on hand to fill the tables with the gardens' abundance, to bring perfect rosebuds for each lady's plate, to provide flower arrangements throughout the house, filling it with beauty and fragrance, was simply imperative, this one time.

Fernande Pierre had asked only once, *"Ce dimanche sera l'occasion unique?"* When Madeline assured her it most certainly was the only such time she would be called away from her family in this manner, she assented willingly enough. She arrived early as usual, standing far down the stone path, looking out over the ocean for a time, and then trotting purposefully about the grounds, her arms and her wheelbarrow laden with clouds of lavenders and crimsons and golds and blues and creams. And when Fernande Pierre, carrying the first of her fragrant burdens, entered the back foyer, careful not to tread farther in her work boots, the house's frantic bustle slowed, lulled to a near peace by armloads of damask roses and lilies of the valley. Trancelike, caterers moved room to veranda to room and back, placing flowers on tables draped in white linen with sterling coming from their centers like the spokes of a wheel.

Fernande Pierre was only to stay until her particular work was completed that morning. Madeline Bradford had made that clear. At 10:30, as the first guests arrived, she could go. But 10:30 came and went and Fernande Pierre did not go, remaining instead in one of the smaller gardens. She had not moved from that place, Madeline noted, since soon after she had brought the last barrowful of roses to the kitchen door.

There she stayed, on her knees, her face nearly touching the earth, up to her dark elbows in darker-still dirt. As though this were an ordinary day. As though this were not a brunch Sunday. Eleven o'clock came and went. The guests began finding seats among the linen-draped tables on the veranda.

In newly painted Adirondack chairs, they sat facing the ocean, where grand views of the sea were framed by the gardens—and by the gardener herself now, bent double and apparently intent upon her dirt.

Madeline watched a moment, noticed how her gardener's Orange Crush T-shirt clashed with the pastel color scheme Fernande herself had so carefully controlled. And the state of the gardener's khakis, soil-stained at the knees, raveling at the bottoms from hems let out, made it look as though she were not sufficiently well paid. Madeline Bradford called to her gardener. Fernande Pierre lifted her head but remained on her knees. *"Oui, madame?"*

"Fernande, I must see you. Come here, please."

Madeline stepped back towards the house, never doubting that her gardener would follow and already beginning to enjoy again the feel of the stiff linen, her new dress, against her legs as she moved.

"Je suis désolé, madame," Fernande said, still digging in the dirt. *"Je ne peux pas."*

Madeline Bradford turned. *"Cannot?* Fernande, pardon me, but I must see you. It is time for you to go home. You've done enough, and I thank you for coming." Madeline Bradford resumed her path to the house.

"Je suis désolé, madame, mais je ne peux pas."

Madeline Bradford turned more slowly this time. "Whatever do you mean 'cannot'? Fernande, did you hear me? It is time for you to *go home.*"

"Je suis désolé, madame. Je ne peux pas. J'ai perdu quelquechose."

"Lost something?" Madeline was becoming aware that yelling across the span of several yards might be noticeable to her guests. She paced halfway to the garden, her face growing tawny, her lips taut (a look she knew to be unbecoming: her ex-husband, of the Beacon Hill brownstone, had often told her so). "Fernande, you can look for that tomorrow. Whatever it is, it will wait. Now, please."

"Je suis désolé, madame," was all the gardener said, not looking at Madeline Bradford and continuing to dig in the dirt.

"Fernande, let me make myself perfectly clear. I am not asking you to leave now. I am insisting. I am your employer, and you desperately need this job, do you not? and I am telling you *it is time for you to go home.* Now."

Fernande Pierre looked up from her dirt without, for a moment, speaking. She remained, though, on her knees. She must not have been thinking about how her husband, Jean Paul, would respond if she lost her job ("playing in the dirt," as he called it), for Fernande Pierre remained unmoved. Turning her attention back to the ground, her face hovered just inches from it. *"Je suis désolé, madame,"* she said from this position, *"mais je ne peux pas. Je cherche ce que j'ai perdu."*

So Madeline Bradford fired her gardener. And so anxious was the hostess of the brunch to retreat— triumphant—from the scene of battle before she might relent to a stubborn, unbending woman with dark-ringed, weirdly unblinking eyes and lips scorched brown by the sun and sea breezes, that Madeline did not see when, just then, Fernande Pierre lifted from the soil a shiny silver coin—a nickel, it seemed. She clutched it tightly and took it with her as she left in the '74 Ford LTD, a contented woman. A woman who did not play. A woman whose back bent and unbent only at her own command.

Amatul Went Back to School

"Six," she said in answer to my fingers
Pawing at the keys. "Six kids: ages
Twelve, ten, five, four, three, two—
And if you have any diapers . . . please."

The *please* was hard for her to mouth:
I saw that in her stiffening chin, the angles
Of her posture sharpening. She looked away
And back again, to see me type her in.

"Sure," I told her, "no big deal, no
Problem, really; we all know things
Are tough, tough breaks, tough times. . . ."
I could not stop my tongue from tapping out

Absurdities, taking from her any choice
To pass me by in silent pride. My fumbling
Words worked no wonders behind her eyes,
Squinting, suspicious, ferocious, kind.

She knew better than I, far better
Than I, where she stood, why I sat:
But she let me pretend to know how she
Felt as the questions I asked got filed by

The date, so we'd know if she came too often.
"No food stamps? But WIC? SSI? Professional
Skills, Amatul?" I said, pronouncing it wrong.
"Rhymes with *school*," she corrected, "And I just

Went back—to school—at night,
Part-time." I nodded, smiled, said the usual
Cheers, but saw in her look not to act
Like I could be her or she could be me,

As though it's all level ground at the
Pitcher's mound, as though some folks
Work hard to stand higher and others don't
Try, and that's how these things are decided.

In the "Comments" line, I typed, "Amatul
Went back to school," then showed her
To the food. She came back each month,
Shoulders slightly less squared, always

Looking away and back to see, or hear, or
Feel if I understood I never possibly could
Understand. She's gone now, on her own now,
With six children: Amatul went back to school.

Mercedes Domingo

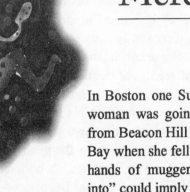

In Boston one Sunday, a woman was going down from Beacon Hill to Back Bay when she fell into the hands of muggers. "Fell into" could imply that she wasn't being wary, that she didn't know the city, didn't know which shadowy folds of antique architecture to skirt, which cobblestone alleyway shortcuts to avoid. But Mercedes Domingo did know the city, knew well the hidden slits of the sleek financial district at midday, knew even better the twilight crooks in the long arms of the city's wharves reaching out into the Inner Harbor.

This Sunday morning early the city streets slept on in undisturbed, self-congratulatory silence. An-

other week of legislation had been passed, another week of derivatives sold, another week of young minds enlightened. So on this day of all days, Bostonians, having nowhere in particular to be, might snooze unmolested until time for brunch.

Mercedes Domingo learned long ago in this town to translate herself into Mercy Davis on job applications and to speak more often of her apartment on Tremont Street than of her home in Honduras. She knew the city well. But her line of work necessitated that she be out when most decent people were in. So on this particular Sunday morning early, as Mercedes—or Mercy, as she sometimes resorted to calling herself—was going down to Back Bay, she fell into the hands of muggers. They took her purse and a good portion of her clothing, and it was hard to say what else: they may have helped themselves to her.

It was a peculiarly gentle mid-March. Boston had already lost its polished white enamel of snow, lost even the black-spattered humps of ice, which typically conducted sit-ins on street curbs and in parking lots until the tulips bloomed.

So here on this mid-March Sunday at the foot of Beacon Hill, the cool, dim tunnels of Park Street subway station steamed with the slow motion of overheated bodies smothered in dark trench coats and down jackets, of people oppressed, prepared for the late-winter freeze that wasn't coming.

One man waiting for a red-line train loosened his wool scarf from his neck, displaying a clerical collar. Perhaps he was trying to avoid the woman in paisley print who was feverishly handing out tracts: rapidly, randomly spraying them about, implanting them like shrapnel. In any case, the clergyman undid his scarf, and this seemed to free him to continue his line of argument and his jelly-filled doughnut, both of which he'd just begun.

"I tell oo, Twom," he said, speaking with his mouth half full, "de whole ihoo"—(he swallowed)—"issue of eternal life is precisely *not* the point. Nothing can be of ultimate human concern which, as Tillich would say, does not have the power of threatening and saving our being. 'Being,' of course, denoting—" he paused to step aside for a Hispanic woman, dirty and scantily clad and dazed, staggering by, *probably drunk,* he thought, then continued—"the whole of reality, of existence."

"No, no, no, no. Jack, Jack, Jack," said his friend, shuffling and reshuffling his sermon notes as a necessary part of his own pre-Sunday worship preparations, a wind-up to the pitch from the pulpit mound. "It is you," he said, "who have missed the point. You and Paul Tillich. To speak of—" The still-staggering Hispanic woman bumped heavily against his arm, causing it to splash hot coffee on his newly laundered coat. "The question of eternal life," he said, snipping off the ends of his words as he wiped coffee from his coat sleeve, "naturally begs the question of salvation, leading inevitably to, as Augustine would have it, *liberum arbitrium liberatum,* the liberated free will—"

"I *know* what it means," said Jack.

"Only then," said his friend, "is humanity capable

of loving God and neighbor, of being even remotely interested in the question 'what must I do to—'"

The Hispanic woman made very little sound when she collapsed against the red tile of the Park Street Station walls, but both men turned toward the fall anyway, so attuned were they to these kinds of disturbances. "A shame," Jack said, shaking his head. "So early in the morning too." He licked the last of the jelly off his fingers. "If faith is to be of relevance today, Tom, it simply must address questions of poverty, violence, questions of—"

The lady in the paisley print, having apparently not exempted Jack from her purposes on account of his clerical collar, marched by shoving a tract—*quite in my face,* he thought, perturbed.

"God loves you," said the woman to the clergymen, "and has a wonderful plan for your life."

Jack gave her a look full of pity—*the laity could be so gullible*—and flicked away the tract as he might have an offending fly. "—Questions of *pain,"* he concluded to his friend.

The lady in the paisley print stepped over to where the Hispanic woman had sunk to the floor, and she peered down into her face, what she could see of it,

its chin dropped flat to the woman's chest. "God loves you," said the pamphleteer, letting a three-color glossy brochure float down into the Hispanic woman's lap, "and has a wonderful plan for your life." The lady sighed and shook her head at the heap on the floor—probably drunk, she knew. "Liquor," she told the red tiles of the Park Street station, "is the devil's own especial tool." With another still-weightier sigh, she turned her offensive towards the fresh troops of tourists just coming down the stairs.

A dark figure drifted in amongst the last wave of those watching for the coming of the Red-Line train. The raised hood of the figure's navy sweatshirt and dark sunglasses left visible only a straight line for a mouth and a nose clearly broken a number of times and deviating to the right. Its hands, too, were hidden by the pockets of black jeans that rumpled down to a stop at black high-tops. It moved forward, its very step a kind of warning, a panther measuring the coiled energy in its legs before a lunge.

"In speaking of loving God and neighbor, Tom," Jack said, moving his wallet from his back pants pocket to the inside front of his suit jacket and pulling a shirt sleeve over his Rolex (a recent gift from his congregation), "we must address ultimates, must forge a new understanding of the daemonic-tragic structures of the human condition as we live it, individually and in community."

The figure passed the clergymen without, apparently, seeing them, then paused, watched them both take an involuntary step backward. For a moment it seemed to enjoy the fear it inspired, fear being the next best thing to respect. But like a cat suddenly bored with its prey, the figure retracted the claws of its hold on the two men and walked away. Jack tugged at his collar, *a little too tight lately,* he thought, and Tom wiped at coffee that was no longer there on his coat sleeve.

A body—inert, not overly clean—curled against the red-tile wall of the Park Street Station caught the dark figure's attention. Approaching warily, leaning down, farther, then farther still, the dark form looked into the woman's face. *"God!"* the figure said to the red-tile walls. "Who is this?"

Jack was surprised the figure had a woman's voice. You never could tell these days. He prided himself on maintaining politically correct positions on current concerns. But there were times (not that he'd risk saying it aloud) when he missed the 1950s of his young manhood, when girls were girls and men were men. And you could tell them apart on the street yards away.

"God!" said the figure again, turning to the crowd this time.

Undaunted by her language, the intrepid pamphleteer stepped from the crowd. "God . . . loves you," she said, "and has a wonderf—"

"Does no one *here know who this is?"* the figure demanded to know, knocking the tract from the lady's hand, sending her arm in a graceless arc around her body. The paisley woman's lips froze into a soundless *O,* her jaw working open and shut like a largemouth bass.

Jack adjusted his clerical collar, wondering now if he would be called upon to intervene. The figure in the hood turned, looking at the crowd that now watched her in silence. She seemed ready to say more, or to make some decisive move in the direction of the crowd waiting for the train at Park Street Station. Instead, she dropped down beside the crumpled bow of the Hispanic woman's body.

Something screamed and Jack jumped, immediately embarrassed to realize it was only the train, the ancient red beast of Boston, coming enraged and screeching from the deep mouth of its tunnel. Jack checked his watch. He was running late. The organist would beat him there again this week. And no doubt she would manage to work that into conversation later.

Jack and his friend and the lady in the paisley print and the rest of the waiting crowd all elbowed one another into position, sidestepping clumsily like half-trained show horses before the doors of the slowing train. All except the figure in the hooded sweatshirt, who stood shouting something at them, mercifully inaudible above the shriek of brakes and rails and metal wheels.

Jack knew the city well, knew its tricks and scams, its clever traps. So the criminal element around Park Street Station was starting to work in concert now. He'd read about the strategy, naturally—the *Globe* was full of such reports—but had not seen it in action before. Jack congratulated him-

self on his street savvy: a less astute observer of urban life might have been taken in.

The two clergymen seated themselves on the Red-Line train just down from the lady in the paisley print. Tom resumed shuffling his sermon notes, which always helped him think more clearly on a Sunday morning early.

"Any consideration, Jack," he said, "of the love of God and neighbor must, as Luther pointed out, be inextricably bound with a basic understanding of divine mer—"

The doors squeezed shut, and the train clattered back into speed. Jack watched as the shouting figure in the hooded sweatshirt shook a dark-knuckled fist at the retreating train. Then the figure turned back towards the unmoving heap of Hispanic woman and leaned down, as though to pick it up.

"Sorry, Tom," Jack said, raising his voice with some effort above the violent hits of steel on steel. "Having trouble hearing. You were saying . . . ?"

ON MOTHERS IN THE 'HOOD

Hear Her Roar

Her girls returned from sledding
Too soon, stuttering, "G-gu—, M-Mom . . ."
"Too cold?" she wanted to know, still
Singing, *When peace like a river attendeth*
My way, when sorrows like sea billows roll,
Without looking up from the stove, where
The water was boiling too fast. Their silence
Made her twist her neck to see her youngest
Crying. "They had . . . ," said the oldest. "Because . . . ,"
Said the second. "They told . . . ," said the third,
While the youngest cried harder still. Their mother
Turned from the stove, forgetting the water boiling
Too fast. "It's too lovely to be indoors today, girls,
With snow just made for tasting, for forts, snowball
Fights, for angels, long rolls down the hill. This is
A day for children to play in." "Guns," said the oldest;

"Boys," said the second; "Mom," said the third;
"They sent us away," said the youngest, who cried.

Their mother turned back to the stove
And stirred, watching steam rise above
The raging beneath. "That's it," she said.
"Too many times. I will not allow it. I will
Not. No longer." *Mom wait, Mom stop, Mom don't,* and
The youngest one clung to her arm. She left her coat
On the hook and her boots by the door when she
Bounded outside, mother bear, at full speed.
"This is a yard," she told the cat on the stoop,
"For children to play in." The cat sharpened its claws,
Watched her go. Her tennis shoes sank in the snow
To her calves. She plunged through it, a tigress
On the attack. The dog slipped from its house to run
Down the hill, lunged on the line at the bottom, and
Barked. *"This is a block,"* she called to the dog, ". . . how
Dare they . . . how *dare* they! . . . *for children to play in."*

Not winded, she reached them, the business
Begun. Too stunned to remember the guns,
They turned, forgetting their deal for the fury
Coming downhill. "Go *away!*" she said, shouting,

"How dare . . . how *dare* you! How dare you intrude
On our homes! Go on back to your own. Out. *Now.*
Too bad you can't stay, but I'm telling you once:
This is a place for children to play in!" They shrank
From her rage, as though they'd been smacked.
They lowered their arms for a moment, stepped
Back. "Sorry," one mumbled, wishing he hadn't
Come today to do business in snow: it was perfect
For sledding, he thought, and fingered his weapon
And longed for the end of his work. His own
Mom would be mad when he came home late
Again, and always with money, too much.

No jacket, no hat, no scarf or boots, she stood
In the snow and watched them retreat, a gang,
With their guns hanging low with their tails,
Turn, surrender the field, slink away. *"This,"*
She yelled to the backs of their jackets,
This is a, This is . . .

    This is a day for
    This is a yard for
    This is a block for
    This is a place for
    This is a world for children to play in!

When Johnnie Sue Got Religion

"They tell you Johnnie Sue tried to kill a man?" Rheba Rhea Baucom asked me first thing.

Someone in town had told me that, in fact. Several sources. I couldn't say just who. One had mentioned a crucifix, I think, and someone else said deer rifle, which seemed to me an unlikely pairing at the scene of a crime—but then I'd been away a long time. There was something, too, about a movie that I didn't quite get either. It was the kind of information—crucifixes and deer rifles and movies and a mother of three trying to kill a man—that just leaks out from under the linoleum and peeks around from behind the cosmetic counter and gets blown about by the ceiling fan in the corner pharmacy when a native wanders back into town asking how everything's been.

I'd known Rheba Rhea Baucom in school all our growing-up years, not well, but well enough to know she could be trusted to store up scraps of town news I might care to gnaw on. Her being thorough with her data and the next door neighbor of Johnnie Sue made Rheba the very person to ask.

But it was not the fact that Johnnie Sue—whom I remembered vaguely from growing up a mile or so away—had tried to kill a man that induced me to ask Rheba Rhea about her my first evening back in town for a visit. At least, what reminded me to ask was less the information itself—intriguing though it was—than the appearance of a dark figure emerging from next door. Its arms were raised, swaying just slightly in the evening breeze like a lone, bare tree, its thick trunk straining up into long, sturdy limbs.

I couldn't help but ask.

Rheba's children—she had four, though in motion they looked and sounded like more—were running through the dusk chasing fireflies as she and I rocked together and drank mint tea on her back porch. "Careful, darlin's," she turned from me to call to them, "careful not to crush their little lights. It's all they got, you know. Without the lights, they's just another ugly bug." She resumed rocking. "So you wanna hear about Johnnie Sue?"

"If you think it's worth the hearing."

"Sugar, I wouldn't waste my breath if it wasn't. 'Course you understand now—I'm not saying I'm the one to ask about Johnnie Sue, seeing as how we never were what you would call close. Divorced. Got herself three boys. 'Bout all I could tell you. . . ."

"That's all I remember from high school days."

"Husband left her years ago for some big-haired blonde Johnnie called the Yellow Buzz Bait—it's a largemouth bass lure, hon. Law, you *have* been away too long. And there were other names: that woman had a mouth on her, Johnnie did."

"Did? But isn't that . . . next door . . . ?"

"Mm-hmm, that's her over there. But I'm referring to before the movie. I'm getting to that. And I do remember—law, who could forget?—she played softball: face got all purple and her hair'd be plastered back flat to her head—looked like a skinned onion—and just cussing the green off the grass. And quite frankly, hon, them kind of fits is pretty near all you need to know about folks, I always said, in a town where the tallest thing still standing is the Presbyterian church steeple."

"I thought it was the Methodists'."

"No, mercy. Ours got blown down, the cross on top did, in a big wind last winter. That was the official word, you understand. I still say the Presbyterians did it theirselves—you know how they can be. And I reckon that's about all I can tell you."

Having known Rheba Rhea since second grade, I remembered enough to keep quiet: sometimes Rheba Rhea thought she'd finished before she was through.

She rocked a while, paused, rocked a while longer, then continued with her story as though she hadn't stopped.

"Well, as her nearest neighbor on the lawn side, not the driveway side, I suppose I could tell you that Johnnie Sue liked messing around with her '74 LTD—largest car known to man—on Saturday mornings early. That was after all us neighbors asked her to find another time for target practice."

"Target practice? With—let me guess—a deer rifle."

"Not bad, darlin', for just back in town. Johnnie Sue used a trash-can lid—a metal one, mind you—for the target. Saturday mornings early. Real early. Tin trash-can lid. Have you *ever?*"

I had not ever, I assured her.

"Mm-hmm. So that's why the LTD, I s'pose. Even the weekends we all slept in, I could always tell she'd been at it again: big, round oil spots on the front lawn and these long white stripes where the tires killed the grass." Rheba Rhea shook her head. "I said to her one time real casual, I said, 'Johnnie Sue, hon, is your pretty yard the very best place for that, do you think?' And she tells me, 'Never can stand to mess up the driveway,' she says and smiles at me like she's real sorry I hadn't thought of that myself. Well, I'm never one to give up easy, so I said to Johnnie Sue, 'What about the garage, sugar? Isn't that where most people do that kind of work, wouldn't you say?' And she tells me most people don't know a fan belt from a garter belt. 'And God help 'em if they did,' she tells me. And then, like this'd explain everything, she says, 'Rebuilt my transmission on the kitchen table one time, but we had to eat off our laps for three weeks.' Like that cleared up the whole thing. So by midsummer every year, Johnnie Sue's yard was just dying of leprosy. Which is why I planted those loblollies over there and that one climbing rose to the right. Block the view, soon's they've grown up big."

I should have known better than to interrupt there, but I had to ask, "What about . . . Why'd she try to kill a man?"

The look Rheba Rhea gave me sent me slumping deeper down into the straw seat of my rocker. "Girl-friend," she scolded, "you have been living up North way, way too long. You are one impatient poodle."

I waited quietly then, just rocking, saying nothing.

Just waiting for the return of her good favor.

"The women in our town," Rheba went on with an air of self-consciously good-tempered long-suffering, "—I'm not saying me, necessarily—tend towards the petite, and what you might call lithe, I'd say."

Certain cues cannot be missed. "You're as slender as ever, Rheba," I told her, one of those obligatory things women say to each other. "Downright willowy," I added, in case I'd happen to forget and interrupt her story again.

"Not like I was in high school, sugar, but for having four children I'll admit I'm not too bad off. And anyway, in the right clothes, you know—this one's a Laura Ashley."

"It's lovely. I just love it," I assured her. And I did. Though I would have said so either way. After all, I did grow up there and still remembered a thing or two about good manners.

Rheba stopped her rocker to smile, not necessarily at me: a diffuse smile that at least included me in its broad beneficence. Then she resumed. "But Johnnie Sue, on the other hand, if you don't mind my saying so, was always built like the packing crate of a major appliance. Square. Solid. And I'm telling

you what, hon, the same dresses on Johnnie Sue looked like she'd gotten tossed in with the flowered sheets during the tumble-dry cycle. And Sundays, that was another odd thing. Sunday around here is a kind of a God and Family Day, you remember, always been that way. But Sundays for Johnnie Sue meant golf. Sundays, she was up early to feed her three boys Lord only knows what—like cold pizza was breakfast—and had chipped her way to the ninth hole by the time we'd all done shaking hands with the preacher.

"Oh," I said politely, the very picture of patience. I was trying hard.

"Well," said Rheba, "one day the preacher over to the Baptist church just got cocky, we all figured. Invited Johnnie Sue to the Easter cantata on a dare from his deacons. Johnnie Sue, she says, 'Why?' Just like that: 'Why?' Which I'd liked to have seen. 'It's Easter,' he tells her. And she wants to know, 'Is the golf course closed this year on Easter?' So he tells her he doesn't think God is best honored on a putting green. And she tells him she's not sure golf is best played from a church pew. And then she offers him a cigarette and says, 'Got a light?' "

"This was before she tried to kill a man?" I asked, forgetting what I was about, distracted by the dark figure swaying in the dusk next door.

Rheba Rhea ignored my question. At least, at the time I thought she was ignoring me. Looking back, maybe she was answering pretty directly given the circumstances: rocking chairs and back porches not having been built with the purpose of getting straight to the point. "If you ask me," Rheba explained carefully, "golf was nothing but an afterthought for Johnnie Sue. Her husband used to play a lot. So I always figured when the folks at the clubhouse said Johnnie Sue was having one of her days (hitting long, hard shots that made the men behind her check their putters, looking for factory defects), she was just picturing that rascal husband of hers and his big yellow lollipop on every ball. She could be nasty in volleyball too—Lord, I've seen it myself—saving her meanest spikes for middle-aged, professional-type men. Right between the eyes. Frank Chauncey, optician over by the fire station—you remember him—used to like to say it took him three summers of men coming in with a bad case of Johnnie Face. Three summers, but he learned. Doubles his stock now every June—men's wire rims, aviator, plastic frames. Doubles it all."

"She must have had some aim," I said encouragingly, "like in her target practice. With the rifle."

Rheba Rhea nodded. "Mm-hmm. But Johnnie Sue's real passion—after rifles and transmissions, maybe—was softball. Behaved like a regular barbarian on the field. Johnnie joined the women's leagues in town, naturally. Problem was she played like a man. Got downright ugly, swearing in languages no one ever'd learned. She just lived for leaving the other side limping and sore. And she swaggered when she won. Swaggered, sure's you're born. So she didn't get to play too much. Not with the men, 'cause they couldn't bear to lose to a woman, you know. And not with the women, 'cause they just couldn't bear . . . Johnnie Sue."

"Oh," I said, but nothing more. Once Rheba Rhea Baucom got cranked up real tight, it was best to just let her go. I relaxed a little lower into my rocking chair and settled in for the ride.

"Lord, then Johnnie got religion when *Jesus Christ Superstar* came to town. She told me she sat on the front row in the Cripple Creek Mall movie theater—it's new is why you don't recollect it. And you know she said to me later, 'Jesus spoke to me then and there.' That's what she told me. Right then. Right there. Large buttered popcorn in hand."

"Jesus' hand?" I was confused.

"*Her* hand, not Jesus'." Rheba turned herself in her chair and leaned towards me, looking me straight in the face, to be sure I was paying attention. "And that's when," she continued, a little louder for my sake, "speaking, at least, as Johnnie Sue's nearest neighbor, that's when I'd say things started changing around here. Really changing."

"Because of a movie? But how did that lead to her trying to kill a—?"

Rheba Rhea held up her hand for silence. "As her nearest neighbor, on the lawn side, I watched Johnnie Sue plant corn all around her swimming pool and tomatoes up the front walk and string beans around the mailbox. That's when things started getting out of hand. Her boys told my boys they wouldn't eat corn or tomatoes or string beans, so Lord only knows what she did with it all. Loaded the food, the corn all shucked and the beans strung, into the LTD every Saturday morning after she got through playing

grease monkey. And somehow, between her house and the golf course, Johnnie Sue got shed of all that haul of vegetables. Maggie Frasier—she runs the Bust-A-Gut now, and I wouldn't recommend nothing but the okra—she thought likely Johnnie Sue sold the corn to the Whitmires. They still do a pretty brisk business, between times the revenuers come in and smash things up."

"They still make that awful stuff?"

"Sugar, they got to—ever since somebody came in telling them they couldn't. But far as Johnnie Sue went, that didn't account for the tomatoes and green beans, I always pointed out to Maggie. So it didn't make walking-around sense the way she figured it. Now Frank Chauncey saw Johnnie hand off bagfuls of something that might or might not have been vegetables one Saturday morning to the pharmacist, Mr. DiGregorio. Frank said maybe she was trading tomatoes for drugs. But Mr. DiGregorio, bless his heart, isn't really bright enough—and Lord knows he's too poor—to be dealing drugs of any kind."

"They still have eight kids, the DiGregorios?"

"Nine, last time I checked. But don't bother asking them: their religion don't allow keeping count.

Anyhow, Johnnie Sue went around saying how she had too much food and had to get rid of it. Got real gruff about it, like she didn't want anybody asking questions, which, you know, is one good way to make sure people do. Meantime, though, Johnnie Sue made a holy mess. Swimming pool started having corn silks floating around on the surface. Sometimes at night, from my back bedroom window I could see the moon shining off that murky water, kind of silver-threaded on the surface, and the corn'd be lit from behind, all black and tall and groping upwards and here would come Johnnie Sue's big, square silhouette, like the creature from the black lagoon. And some nights she'd stand there looking like the corn, straight and tall, and swaying with her arms up like she was reaching for something she couldn't quite touch."

"Like now."

"Like now. Only she started it a while back. And then weekend nights, Johnnie Sue started having these parties: loud affairs with lots of food, mostly burgers on the grill, and too many people in the pool—some of them fully clothed, from what I could see. Place'd be lit up like she owned the power plant, and all sorts of characters I'd never seen before'd be coming and going all hours. I never was invited to any of these functions, and neither were any of the people I knew. Not even the kind of people I knew. Oh, I did see Benjy Meeks there once—you remember him from school, bless his heart, never did finish. He's a mechanic now down to the BP."

"How is ol' Benjy Meeks?"

"He'd tell you he's got nothing to complain about, though between you and me, there's not much to brag about either. And there was one of Johnnie Sue's parties I saw Marty at—"

"Marty?"

"He's our garbage man—I wouldn't know his last name. Saw him over there once or twice too. That kind of people showed up. You know. Well, one time I asked Marty—he's a black man, but generally real honest—I said, 'Marty, things surely are strange over to Johnnie Sue's.' 'Yes'm,' he says back. 'Yes'm, they sure are,' he tells me, just grinning. So I told him, I said, 'I bet if a body wanted to, he could tell just a whole lot from a look at people's trash.' And he tells me 'Yes'm.' He said to me, 'Yes'm, trash tells a lot.' Just like that and laughs like it was some

117

big secret. So he wasn't much help. And there was one party where the husband showed up."

"The husband?"

"Bobby. Johnnie Sue's husband, you know, that left her for the dandelion. That was something. She smacked him across the face but good, pushed him in the pool—just shouting away at him that if he ever came back she'd a good mind to kill him. Everybody heard. *I* heard, and I was just sitting way over here minding my own business."

"So that was when she tried to kill—"

"Law, no. Not that time. But let's just say it didn't look good, her threatening him like that in front of God and everybody. Well, then she ran in the house crying—nobody'd ever seen her cry before, so that was something too. And with the husband all soggy in the pool, well, that particular party ended early."

"When was that?"

"Just after Johnnie Sue announced Jesus Had Met Her, large buttered popcorn in hand. Her hand."

"But this was before the deer rifle gets dusted off again?"

"That's after the spring revival and her going over to the Catholics. Understand now, I've got nothing against religion. Or Catholics, either one."

"'Course not."

"Well, you know, down to the Methodist church we're still convinced John Wesley's watching from some air-conditioned sky box in heaven. So we keep with the yearly revival, though we try to work it a little more sophisticated—you know, so nobody goes hanging their conscience out to dry in public. And then, too, it's been trimmed from two weeks to one after the winter we lost the cross off our steeple—thanks either to a particularly violent act of God or to the Presbyterians' being jealous. You know how they can be. But wouldn't you know, Johnnie Sue just loved it."

"The steeple?"

"The spring revival, hon."

"Oh. Of course."

"You remember about revivals. They're all alike, every blessed one. Doreen—been our organist ever since Jonah met the whale—she always plays 'Just As I Am' so many times through you'd reckon we'd got hit on the head and gone Baptist. But we all know how to keep our seats. I just always sit there wishing the revival preacher—they're all alike too, bless 'em—would go wash that goop out of his hair, go have hisself a Coke out back under the trees and cool down for a while. I never can bear seeing a preacher sweat right through his undershirt, and all flailing and thrashing about like he'd up and drown right there if somebody didn't quick give their lives to Jesus."

I nodded, letting the back and forth, back and forth of the porch chair rock me gently out of the present. "I haven't thought about the spring revivals in years," I told Rheba Rhea. "You don't see too much of them up North," I added. I'd forgotten, or maybe just had no reason to recall until then, those big tent preachers from my youth: how every now and then, one would get entirely out of control and start the old-time tent-meeting pitch and roll: the big march forward ("God has told me"), the charge up the hill ("that there is one person"), then over the top ("here tonight who") and the slide to the bottom ("needs to know Jesus") with a lift on the last syllable, signaling the preacher's willingness to repeat the whole thing over—and over— 'Til folks got so scared he'd have a coronary on us, they went on down front just to save the old boy from himself. Though after the standard six verses sung of the closing hymn, then three times through organ only, nobody much cared anymore about saving the preacher. A couple of the deacons would stand up conspicuously in the back and march out to unpack the ice-cream churns from their station wagons and set up tables on the church lawn. And so we generally were spared the indignity of excess emotion and managed to get ourselves out of worship early enough for us kids to catch fireflies in back of the old parsonage and eat hand-churned peach ice cream 'til we couldn't move to catch the fireflies anymore.

I watched Rheba's children, now on their back lawn tumbling over one another, diving and clutching, pawing and peering at the little lights dancing in the dusk, and calling to each other to, quick, bring the jar, grab the lid. "So . . . ," I said, turning to Rheba slowly, still on my way back from the past, "so Johnnie Sue loved the spring revival."

"You might've known, just fresh converted by a Hollywood movie most of us either weren't allowed to go see or couldn't figure out how to go without being seen. It was bad enough she had to hug all over anything that moved. But then she took to the second pew back on the right, which, you know, might as well be sitting on the preacher's lap. Then, one evening, she went and did it."

"Tried to kill a man? The preacher?"

"Not that yet. There's still the Catholics. She raised her hands during the closing hymn. *Above her head*. Right there, in front of God and everybody. Well, trying to make light of it, the head usher, Charlie Slater, said, 'Maybe she's limbering up for the volleyball season.' But we knew better. And Benjy Meeks said that he looked the same way when he checked out people's cars up on the rack, but somebody said—and 'course I knew for a fact—he'd been seen over to one of Johnnie Sue's cookouts, so you'd have to figure he'd be sticking up for her. Reenie, she's my oldest, told me later the high school cheerleaders made up a pom-pom routine that featured a real darling Johnnie Sue move. And now and then at the club, a golfer playing under par would raise his hands and face to the sky and wriggle—and we all knew what he meant and where he learned the steps."

"Doing the Johnnie Sue."

"Mm-hmm. Well, if you can imagine, night after blessed night during the spring revival, Johnnie Sue raised her arms to sing, and she wept, just blubbered. Loud, too. Comes to the very front and tells the preacher—law, I about fell off my pew—that she'd like prayer that she wouldn't want to kill her husband."

"Former husband?"

"Whatever, sugar. But that was Johnnie's idea of a prayer request: Lord, stop me just this side of murder, please. And by Sunday morning you'd have thought Johnnie Sue was a permanent fixture on that second-row pew. Whatever energy used to get released cussing and playing softball and cussing and playing golf, it got channeled into these eerie moans. Like a cow in heat, if you ask me. During the time of silent meditation, when Doreen was supposed to let the organ drone real quiet, Johnnie Sue's commotion had us all squirming in our seats, looking around for what poor creature got caught in the organ pipes. The holy in the air got ruined, needless to say. And we'd all just sit there looking at each other and looking at Johnnie Sue and wishing the clergy knew when they was beat."

"Clergy'd be the last to know."

"Well, after service one Sunday, I was standing

right behind Johnnie Sue in the line where you have to shake the pastor's hand and say 'nice sermon' or 'Lord blessed' or 'Spirit moved in a powerful way'— when he pulled Johnnie aside. He couldn't have been nicer. Just explained how things were. And standing right there I couldn't help but hear. He said, 'Bearing in mind your admirable devotion to Christ, of course, I wonder if it might not be possible that your particular . . . style of worship might not be making other less . . . physically involved worshipers uncomfortable.' You got to give the man credit for trying. I'm telling you what, though, Johnnie Sue looked then like my cousin Lamar—you remember the time we were kids, getting his horse's front leg unstuck from out the cattle crossing: all of a sudden shot loose, landed in his face."

"How is his face these days?"

"I don't know but what a little rearranging didn't improve it some in the long run. But Johnnie Sue, she told the preacher then, 'I figure I just might be freeing inhibited souls.' Well, he agreed, you know. Pretty amiable about it too. Said she might eventually do just that. 'But,' he said, 'some souls here look a whole lot better inhibited.' "

"He makes a point."

"Well, but Jesus had met her, Johnnie Sue said. And she wouldn't back down. And then, him being big pals with the Catholic priest across town (they play golf together every Friday after hospital visits— always pulling pranks on each other), the pastor suggested to Johnnie Sue that the Catholic church had a real nice tradition of mystics: people who were different, like her, about how they talked to God— most all either real loud or didn't say nothing at all, ever, on purpose."

"How'd she take it?"

"Who ever could tell with Johnnie Sue? But she went on over to the Catholics: every square inch of her. Be standing in the grocery store in front of the frozen foods and all of a sudden start beating her chest, saying, 'Through my fault, through my fault, through my most grievous fault.' Like the filet of fish are there to hear confession. She'd tell the boys bagging the food, 'God of God, light of light, true God of true God, begotten not made . . . ," and the boys made a game of it, learned the chant and made up hand motions. The cashiers, though, they got nervous. Made them miss a key when she'd start in on 'We beseech thy mercy,' and all they could say was 'Got any coupons?' Johnnie Sue showed up for every mass. Never missed a confession. And never quit with the hands-above-the-head thing or the crying out loud. Or the cookout parties either. The priest showed up to one or two of her parties. Once or twice that I saw. And then, he came back."

"The priest?"

"The husband, sugar. Former husband."

"Oh. Oh, my. So here it comes."

"Well, Bobby came back. Which he should have known not to. But he came strolling up her front sidewalk like he owned the place, which he technically might still have, I don't know. But imagine the nerve.

"'Howdy, hon,' he hollers up the drive. *Hon.* Imagine. And then he calls her some things must've been pet names—Foxy Moxie Mama and Lady Long Legs and Big Angel Babe and some I'd rather not repeat. You know, he was making as much money as ever, from what the boys at his plant said, and none of us had seen the Little Yellow Buzz Bait around in forever and a day, so you might've thought Johnnie Sue'd give him at least a hearing. But Lord knows I could hear her next door, even with the air on. She started *making up* vulgar names for him once she ran out of what you might call standards. Well, Johnnie Sue's husband, he came out of that house moving like a leopard with his spots shot off. I tell you what: Johnnie Sue riled up woulda put the fear of God in anybody else. But Bobby just laughed, looking over his shoulder, running. Johnnie Sue came out after him like a stampeding bull, and throwing things: eggbeater, softball glove, tennis shoe, things I couldn't even make out, all bouncing off him onto the driveway, which was wet that morning (but Lord knows it was free of oil spots). And him just laughing at her. So she let him have it."

"The rifle!"

"The cross, darlin'. Johnnie Sue'd taken to wearing one of them Howdy-See-My-Silver-Jesus kind of crucifixes ever since she went over to the Catholics. Well, sugar, Johnnie Sue ripped that chain clean off her neck and sent it flying. Just flying. Hit that man right between the eyes like she was hunting buck. Bounced off onto the driveway, lying next to the eggbeater."

"Was he still laughing?"

"Law, hon, Bobby's not real bright, but he'd caught on by then. He leans over to pick up the necklace, and I think he mighta handed it back to her almost civil. If she hadn't of shot him then."

"Shot him handing her back her crucifix?"

"Shot him bending over to get it, clean through between his legs like he was a croquet mallet. Scared him so bad he dropped the thing cold. Then she let go two more. Which was when I called the police, telling them to come quick, Johnnie Sue was trying to kill a man. And Boyd Veal, he was the one on duty, says to me, 'Rheba, you're talking to a man who's played volleyball with Johnnie Sue. Tell me something I don't know.' Well, I straightened him out good, and they came on. 'Course Bobby, he was long gone by then."

"He could still drive?"

"Faster'n ever. Johnnie Sue'd shot off that man's belt loops on either side, maybe lost him a few more hairs off the dome, but nothing you need a stretcher for. 'Course that didn't take care of the fact she'd tried to kill a man."

"You can't have that kind of thing in a civilized place."

"Well, after Bobby left but before the police got there, I watched Johnnie Sue from the kitchen window. She sat there in the driveway, kind of collapsed in this heap of golf shirt, tennis shorts, and knee-high tube socks—with, you know, those big red stripes at the calves, didn't match the shirt or shorts either one. The driveway was all wet, like I said, but she just sat right down, put the softball glove in her lap and the necklace on her knees and her face on the necklace and her hands just tearing at the glove like she wanted to shred the leather by hand. Just cried and cried and cried, saying so I could barely hear her, 'Thanks be to . . . thanks . . .' the entire time, like all that axle grease'd finally sunk one cog too far. So now, you must be sitting there watching her next door and wondering how come a character like that is loose on the streets."

"I'm guessing the judge'd played volleyball with Johnnie Sue before."

"I tell you what, it was that cookout crowd. Every blessed one had something to say to the police. Benjy Meeks showed up testifying how Johnnie Sue is one fine shot with a deer rifle: if she wanted to kill a man, she would have gone and done it. And Marty, my garbage man I mentioned before, he passed around the trash-can lid Johnnie used for target practice and talked about the math, showed by how far back she stood to practice, and how short a range as Bobby was from her, he wouldn't have had a prayer, or anything else, if she'd been aiming. And then the priest went and made himself a character witness, talking all about how she had a good heart."

"Did he come back?"

"The priest?"

"The husband. Former husband. Former husband short two belt loops."

"Well, in the end, I tell you what, Bobby never would press charges. Never backed down from saying Johnnie Sue'd wanted to kill him either, but never would press charges. So there was nothing to do but for Boyd Veal to take the rifle away and give the crucifix back and tell Johnnie Sue to try to behave herself."

I nodded, squinting to see the figure next door. Dusk eased into a darkness that hid her from us. "And has she?"

"Well, hon, word gets around in a small town, so I don't know if it's more that she's behaved—or if most of us just steer clear of her. We let Johnnie Sue alone to raise her hands above her head and weep in public and tilt her face back towards heaven—just as she pleases. Over to the Catholic church, they mostly just explain to newcomers, sometimes let them figure it out for theirselves."

We rocked a while in silence. It was too dark now to see if the figure next door still stood reaching, stretching, straining up, trying to touch something somewhere beyond the back yard of a small suburban town.

The captured little dancing lights in Rheba's children's jar flickered dimly.

Rheba's voice was slowing, pulling up to dock. "I've heard, though," she said in the deeper hum of a motor geared down now to nearly idling, "that sometimes smack in the middle of the 'Our Father' when it's real quiet, you know, the fits'll come on Johnnie Sue, like a horse with colic. And there she is just weeping. Except now she cries aloud in Latin, which I guess just goes to show you." Rheba shifted then, with only a little lurch backward, into silence.

I nodded again and ceased rocking and stretched my legs out full length, letting Rheba Rhea know I knew she'd reached the end of her answer to my question.

"Kids, ya'll come on up, hear?" Rheba Rhea called to her children, barely visible now through the sorghum of a humid, Southern summer night.

They obeyed reluctantly, as all children turn grudgingly from their day's-end games. The two oldest lagged last, capturing one or two final fireflies in their hands, peeking inside the cages of their palms cupped together to where, inside, the tiniest bulb blinked on and off, on and off. In the end, of course, they promised to let all the fireflies go free— though every now and then, I couldn't help but think, one might still get crushed in that greedy excitement of children playing in the dark, chasing after those little bitty pinpricks of light.

ON MENTAL ILLNESS

Some of My Best
Friends Are Crazy

One of my best friends is crazy,
By which I do not mean
    she
Spends her last ten bucks in the world
     (this month)
      On a baseball cap
       with eyelet trim or
Composes songs over
     the phone though
     She cannot
      sing—and knows it—or
Wears sneakers in the snow
      with pink socks.

She's done that, of course, but that's not
        what
I mean when I say she's
        crazy.

I mean what *she* says: she's
        nuts.
Sometimes, that is. Or maybe (I
        don't know),
Maybe always
        crazy, just
Aided by doctors and drugs—and by
        Jesus, she says.

I did not know my friend when
        she was a child,
When her loved ones did not . . .
        love her—
By which I mean
        nobody
Should treat a child like that.
        No body.

I did not know my friend when
      she slept, or didn't,
In shelters that were
      not—
Places with cots and walls that kept out
      wind but
Could not offer warmth.
      No home.

I know my friend as she is
      now
Five decades full
      of youth almost
Who knows all the right people:
      street folk, disabled;
Who oversees an office
      though
She cannot
      spell—and knows it;
Who snaps the place into
      place, and
Earns surprised respect,
      everyone's.

I know my friend as she is
     now—
With sufficient funds for groceries
     only,
For the party she'll throw
     this month
For friends. Enough
     for that and for
Her gift: plush pink and green
     with the head that bows and
Twists and plays a tune to
     make my daughter laugh:
Baby's first toy—and
     best.

I know my friend as she's
     become:
The first to call when I
     was sick,
When doctors couldn't say
     why.
The one who called when she
     was ill

To say she'd be awhile in the
        nuthouse,
She said, and to
        please
Pray
        for the doctors and the drugs.

So I said,
        Jesus,
Some of my best friends are
        crazy.

Sanctuary

She could see out her car window—though barely, given its thick yellow-gray filter of fine-powdered pollen and granulated road grime—the beginning of one of the paths that led down to the creek. And she could see better still in her mind the way the sunlight came stippled through the trees and lay gently on the moss incline of the stream's broad banks. When she remembered that place on the creek—which wasn't so often anymore—she recalled less about herself or her neighborhood friends or the games they'd played there than she did that way the light came down in grainy golden shafts, refracting off the water onto their own summer-freckled faces, onto the mountain laurel beside the creek, onto the shy white undersides of the old oak leaves.

"Sugar, stop the car here . . . if you think we have time." The backs of her thighs squeaked against the vinyl. Lila leaned across the seat to touch her husband's forearm, its blond carpet of hair wrapping round to a meaty underside. His forearms alone, she'd often thought, were thick as baseball bats, the part that did the hitting. She looked at his arms: his T-shirt sleeves edged with the end of the brown skin and the beginning of the white. She'd never known him, even in the very dead of winter, not to have tan lines at his neck and upper arms. J.P. spit into his cup, half full now of brown juice from the snuff distorting his bottom lip. Taut and thick-swollen looking, Lila thought, the way Novocain at the dentist's office felt.

"Thought you said she's expectin' us at three," he said. "What time you got?"

He'd never worn a watch, not in the time she'd known him anyhow. And that was—she calculated twice to be sure, its seeming longer than she'd remembered—a good seventeen years now. Met when she was sixteen and married right out of high school. And low and behold, here she was thirty-three, still telling him what time it was.

"Well, I did. I did tell her that. And it's three now. I just wanted . . . , these woods we used to play in growing up. I wanted to show the children."

"Not if you wanna be on time, you don't."

She watched the entrance to the path go by. "Then maybe afterwards."

"You don't think the kids seen enough trees in their lives? Like we hadn't got seven acres of 'em out behind the house. Lord, woods is woods, Lila."

"It's not that." She took her hand from her husband's arm and began fiddling with her door handle. "I just thought . . . That's her house, on the right there. The white one. You can turn—"

"I seen the driveway."

Lila turned around to wake a groggy back seat. "Kay Lee, honey, you got your shoes on, sugar? Jabo, help your sister find her shoes. Don't jostle the baby, Jabo. Law, he didn't sleep all afternoon. Don't wake him up now, for heaven's sakes."

"Momma, Jenks spit up on hisself again."

"Momma, Jabo's hidin' one of my shoes. Give it back! I want my shoe! Give it!"

"Tattletale."

"Big-Headed Brat."

"'Least I don't got a big—"

"Shut up," J.P. told the back seat.

Jabo leaned over to his sister to whisper in her ear, "Cry baby."

"Momma, did you hear—?"

J.P. turned off the ignition with a snap of his thick wrist. "I thought I told you to shut up," he said. Without turning around to see what he might come in contact with, he swept his right arm across the back seat like a tree limb just let loose from being pinioned way back out of its natural line. Kay Lee wailed.

Recoiled to the far corner of the front seat, Lila

let her husband climb out of the car first. He'd be needing to slam the door while she was still inside. Lila reached first for the baby, awake now and crying too. "Hush now, Jenks, honey. Katydid, you're alright, sweetheart. You're alright now. Jabo, take my hand. Let me look at your cheek. You're alright now. It'll be okay, baby. How 'bout helpin' your sister? Miss Lacey's expectin' us. We don't want her to think something's wrong, now do we?"

Wiping his tears with first one shoulder and then the other, Jabo unbuckled his seat belt and reached over to unstick Kay Lee's. "Don't cry, Kay," he whispered. "You're okay. He got me not you anyhow. Don't cry. I'm sorry."

Lila unfastened the infant seat and with the two older children in her wake and the youngest one's carrier slung over her arm, she followed her husband up the driveway, two parallel concrete tracks between which timothy grass and dandelions flourished undiscouraged, to Hazel Lacey's house.

Hazel had already seen them coming and was across the porch and down the stairs before Lila could remind the children of their manners in a stranger's house.

Hazel Lacey was a wisp of a woman who smelled faintly of lavender and faintly of cedar and faintly of fried onion rings, from which, she said, she never could refrain, not even when the doctor explained to her back in the 70s about cholesterol and showed her some numbers he'd claimed were hers—her cholesterol's. She'd smiled and nodded and dropped by the Dairy Queen for the usual order on the way home.

Breezing past J.P. like a sailboat on a broad reach, the winds off her beam, Hazel headed now for Lila with both arms out. The loose, wrinkled skin of her upper arms dangled down in turkey-chin folds that looked as though they might just wriggle free of the bone any moment. "Why, Lila Fairbanks, you are back at last."

"DeWeese," J.P. said. "Lila DeWeese."

Hazel Lacey pivoted on the toe of one Reebok to acknowledge J.P.'s existence, then continued on towards her object. So thin in her blue cotton house dress, she looked, Lila thought, like a Q-tip: cottonball hair at one end, size-9 white sneakers at the other.

"Little Lila Fairbanks, come home—and with

three of the prettiest chickies I do believe I have *ever* seen. And you, young lady, must be . . ."

"Kay Lee Jackson DeWeese," the child told her, sticking out her hand tentatively, like a kitten's paw feeling its way. "And I'm eight," she added, because adults always asked that next.

Hazel Lacey shook the child's hand vigorously. "You favor your momma in looks, Kay Lee Jackson DeWeese, and if you're half as smart, I'll count myself proud to know you."

Kay Lee beamed. The little girl's brother took charge then, stepping forward with hand up, shoulders back. "I'm Jonah Paul DeWeese Junior. But you can call me Jabo. I'm the oldest."

Hazel Lacey turned towards him, the laughter in her cheeks pushing her eyes into blue slits. "So pleased to meet you both, Kay Lee and Jabo. And this one swinging on his momma's muscles must be little Jenks," said Hazel, giving the baby some semblance of a wave on her way to hugging its mother around the neck. "My *heavens,* it's good to see all you all. Welcome *home."* Hazel Lacey turned now and smiled at J.P. There was a certain refinement about Hazel Lacey when she smiled, Lila decided.

Something like the cool sheen of well-polished pewter: simple, solid, elegant.

"'Fraid home's up Tullahoma way now to all us here, ma'am," J.P. said. "But it's nice to be back in these parts again. Been awhile."

Lila stepped out from behind her children. "Hazel Lacey, I'd like you to meet my husband, J.P. DeWeese. His people used to live down in the valley, out by Missionary Ridge, before his daddy retired from the DuPont plant and moved. Up our way."

Hazel held out a hand, long and white, its skin nearly translucent, delicately boned, but with a grip on which she'd always prided herself. It made, she'd found, strong men open their eyes a little wider when they said "how do you do" to her.

"Cleanin' trout and cannin' peaches for sixty, seventy years," she told J.P. before he asked. "The jar I can't open myself hasn't yet been made. Glad to make the acquaintance of Lila Fairbanks's husband after all these years. You must be thirsty. Just finished the lemonade—only blessed thing I can make in the kitchen without settin' off the smoke alarm—and, Jabo, if you'd help me serve it. Kay Lee, you're a wiry one. You want to skedaddle on inside and pull over one more chair from the far end there?"

Hazel ascended her steep porch steps like a mountain climber, using the wooden railing to haul herself upward, leaning slightly backward, moving quickly. She was halfway up before J.P. thought to offer her his arm and up entirely before she said, "Why, thank you, J.P., but I'm fine. Just fine."

They all helped Kay Lee gather the white wicker porch furniture into a semicircle while Jabo struggled with an overfull pitcher and five stemmed glasses swaying as he set them down. Lila steadied one or two on their way over.

"Why don't you tell me all about life in Tullahoma now," Hazel said. "Everything an old, old—holy Moses, I'm old—friend of the family needs to know. Everything important. You children have a dog?"

"Mine's Buddy," said Jabo, bouncing forward in his seat. "Hers," he nodded towards his sister, who was also sitting forward now, "is Milky Way. Not much of a name for a dog, me 'n' Dad done tol' her. But you can't tell that girl noth—"

"Milky Way's a heap smarter 'n Buddy ever thought about bein', Little Ja-Bo Peep. Just ask Momma, she knows."

Jabo kicked one sneakered foot that fell just short of its aim—his sister. "Like you'd know about smarts. And I thought I told you not to call me—"

"They're mutts," Lila offered. "Real sweet dogs, both of them."

"Dumb as stumps, both of 'em," said J.P. "Gunshy's rabbits."

"Doesn't mean they're stupid," Lila said to her lemonade. Hazel Lacey reached over to pour her more.

"Tell me about what you big people are up to," Hazel said, trotting to the screen door and reaching inside for a tray of Club crackers and cream cheese with pepper jelly.

"Daddy's just switched jobs over to the high school," Jabo told Hazel Lacey.

"First winnin' season since Adam got his rib stole," J.P. said. "Lookin' to get moved up here before long. Head coach ain't worth much."

"I ain't never missed a game," Jabo said, bouncing in his seat. "I know all the plays and all th—"

Grinning, J.P. simultaneously spit into the cup and whapped a big hand on his son's back, knocking the boy slightly off balance on one bounce. "Clear shot

137

better 'n some a my tight ends."

Lila reached for more cream cheese and pepper jelly without looking up, then proceeded to study the pepper-jelly label. "We can't get this in Tullahoma," she said when she realized Hazel Lacey was watching her.

"Couldn't here either if I didn't wish for it real bad, click my heels together three times, and tell the store manager I'm chaining myself to the toilet-tissue display until he finds me some. Now what about you, Lila, hon? What're you up to?"

"Me? Oh, I don't know. I stay busy. Ever since Jenks came along I don't seem to have time to see straight. I been thinking some about going back to school when the kids get—"

J.P. snorted. Hazel Lacey turned blue eye slits on him that looked, Lila thought, especially remote these days in sockets sunk deeper than she'd remembered.

Lila said nothing for a moment, then addressed the pepper jelly, "The children won't be little forever."

Kay Lee left her seat and wrapped her arms around her mother's neck from behind the white wicker chair. "Don't leave us, Momma."

Lila reached back to stroke her daughter's head. "Momma's not leaving you, sugar."

"I always thought, Lila, hon," said Hazel Lacey, pouring her more lemonade, "that you had the most extraordinary gift of teaching. You mind all those afternoons down by the creek?"

Kay Lee circled the chair to perch in her mother's lap. "What'd Momma do down by the creek, Miss Lacey? Were you there?"

"I visited a time or two when I was specially invited, sugar. And times of year the leaves were off the trees I could see a little." Hazel leaned towards the children, "Nosy old ladies just love to watch what's going on behind their creaky old backs."

Lila reached out a hand to pat Hazel's spindle of an arm. "You just watched to see when we were headed your way—don't act like we didn't know."

"I never."

"This sweet lady you see here before you," Lila told her children, "would watch to see when we'd finish playing down by the stream. Every time we'd head up the path, there she'd be, brown paper sack in hand, acting like she'd just come back from the grocery: just happenin' to always have bought more banana Popsicles than she could eat."

"I always had a freezer too small. Been my one regret in life. At this very minute, I tell you, I am plagued with Popsicles—*plagued*, I tell you. They will most certainly lie on this very porch and melt tonight—and suffer in the process—if some kind soul doesn't help me." Hazel Lacey turned to Kay Lee. "I wonder if you'd—"

"I'll help you," said Jabo, still bouncing in his seat and now springing clear out of it. "I'll help you, Miss Lacey."

Kay Lee nodded and slid off her mother's lap, making no sound when her sandals met the porch's wooden planks. "Me too, Miss Lacey?"

Hazel Lacey turned at the door to her living room. "There's just one condition. No dripping in the house. Or on the porch, come to think of it. Your momma can tell you I have taken religious vows against housework. And yard work. Yard won't do either for drips. My ants are god-awful aggressive this time of year. I thought maybe down by the creek'd be nice. You children need to see where your momma held her classes."

J.P. spit brown saliva into his cup, fast approaching full.

"Your momma," Hazel Lacey told the children, "was the smartest thing people'd seen around here since—well, since I was her age, I s'pose," she decided cheerily.

"You'll notice," Lila smiled slowly, "she didn't say prettiest. Hazel, you can tell me now. Was I as ugly a child as I recall? All teeth with two big braids attached?"

"You weren't . . ." Hazel Lacey paused to consider. "You weren't near's pretty then as you got." She nodded, pleased with her own diplomacy. "Whatever homely you had, child, you made up for with heart. Your momma," she addressed the children again, "would round up the pagan hordes playing Red Rover and Hide-and-Seek back in these woods and she would set them down like they was her congregation, like she was the only thing standing between them and the bottom circle of hell." Hazel chuckled, a low bubbling sound, and looked out beyond her front porch, far into the woods, as though if she watched closely, she might see the little gatherings even now. "Your momma made little games, mazes and dot-to-dots, for the ones that couldn't read, little games she made herself, and then she'd give her sermons on Finding the Way Home. Had these long braids back then, color of straw and stiff as two broomsticks, big bows on the ends, swung back and forth when she got excited, now and then hit her clean in the face. Best little—"

"Married me a *preacher,*" J.P. roared, spitting into his cup this time with a force that splashed brown juice out onto his hand.

"Best little preacher you ever saw," Hazel Lacey told the children. "Day I find one around here good's her is the day I call church worth puttin' my panty-hose on for." She laid one hand on each child's shoulder and steered them in an about-face. "Now you folks wander on down—"

J.P. was laughing so hard he choked on the latest gathering of brown spittle. "Hear that? Bucktoothed little preacher had my babies for me!" He wheezed, his face going deep red with the humor of it all. "Bucktoothed little preacher with big bows on her braids!"

"Wander on down to the woods now," said Hazel Lacey. "All ya'll go on. Do you good. I'll keep baby Jenks up here with me. Sound asleep—he'll be fine. Just fine. You all run along now. Time's awastin'. I'll bring the Popsicles on down directly."

Jabo sloshed lemonade, transferred into a paper cup, all the way down the path leading from Hazel Lacey's front porch into the woods. The same sun that had cut hot triangles through the car windows all the way down from Tullahoma melted now into soft yellow light, filtered by a canopy of dogwoods leaning like young mothers, solicitous, lithe, out over the moss banks of the creek. Rough-barked branches of the chestnut oaks, broad shouldered, imposing, thrust themselves over and across the dogwoods, streamward.

Jabo, his lemonade drained, had shed his sneakers, rolled up his jeans and waded in before Lila, the last one down the path, reached the stream. "A-a-agh, it's cold! Momma, it's so cold!" he yelled, already up to his knees.

"Is it, 'Bo, honey? I think it always—"

"You sound like a stuck girl pig in there squealin'. Be a man about something for a change," his father told him. "Mountain streams is like that. Cold's what they are." J.P. DeWeese worked another wad of snuff under his bottom lip—preferring it to lemonade any old day, he'd told Hazel Lacey. "More for us," she'd said, smiling her polished-pewter smile.

Mountain stream, Lila thought. Here in East Tennessee where the land buckles up like blistered paint. But the natives chose to call them mountains, these hills stumbling down off the Appalachian chain, because their daddies did—and their daddies' daddies before them. So mountains they were.

And this particular stream, Lila observed to herself, letting her mind meander forward with the current, this stream flowed along caring nothing either way—mountains or hills. It merely followed its course to the cliffs over by Falling Water, with its impending 2,000-foot drop to the valley below. *Brave little stream,* Lila thought. *Stupid, stupid stream.*

Kay Lee had by now unbuckled her sandals, trusting their protection to the hollow trunk of a chestnut oak. Feeling the moss for a dry place, she seated herself at the creek's edge. From her winter-soft soles little by little to her ankles, she let her feet be washed by the frothy reach of the stream's surface.

Nothing much has changed here, Lila thought,

slipping off her own shoes to feel the wet red clay slip between her toes. The sweet gum and red maple and white oaks, they were all still here too, silent, but swaying their raised arms slightly in the soft wind, like the faithful at prayer.

Jabo had ceased his exclamations over the water temperature and stood still, studying a tiny cove formed by two big rocks, where a water bug was suspended, its delicate stilted legs strong and stable on the stream's taut surface.

Lila wandered over to the concrete tunnel that conducted the stream under Fairmont Street. Beside the tunnel, a granite boulder cleft by the long-ago violence of the road's construction formed a small, shallow cave. Lila crawled inside, feeling the clammy cool wrap round her. Above her, below her, and on either side, she could see nothing but rock. Only straight ahead could she see out, and then only her children, both utterly absorbed in their surroundings. Kay Lee was humming softly, kicking her bare feet back and forth across the stream's filmy surface in time to her song, randomly shifting tempo here and there and occasionally changing key. The child had a pleasing voice, Lila thought, a sweet, pure sound, if a bit too reedy, too fragile.

Lila could hear J.P. pacing back and forth on the stream's bank. "Woods is woods," he spat, sending brown juice in her direction. "I told her woods is woods. Bucktoothed b—"

Lila couldn't hear the rest. Didn't need to. And not being able to actually see him from her cleft of rock, Lila didn't mind somehow. Didn't even bother to respond when he lobbed her way, "I'm headin' up to the car." She could hear his pacing stop, could feel his body braced for her reaction. When none came, twigs on the path snapped and branches whipped against each other, pulled back, let fly, pulled back, let fly.

Neither Jabo nor Kay Lee stirred at their father's exit. Jabo followed his bug's walk on water. Kay Lee continued her tune, beginning to add lyrics now: a line here, a word or two there.

On one side of the stream grew cattails, their long, slender green stems stirring in the breeze. As children, Lila remembered, the boys loved to pick the cattails in early fall just as their fuzzy brown heads were near bursting. By breaking the stems at their bases, they made the cattails into swords, beating the brown heads at one another until the soft skins split, spilling white feathery stuffing like the flyaway flower of a dandelion.

Honeysuckle grew wild along the far bank. Its scent filled the little clearing as incense fills a cathedral. Jabo picked one of the flowers, presented it to his sister and immediately retreated, fearful of appearances.

"C'm 'ere, 'Bo," Kay Lee said, omitting any thank-yous for the sake of his pride. The boy came. "You ever tasted the honey inside?" She pulled the little flower's stamen out, holding the dripping base for her brother's outstretched tongue. "Taste and see," she said.

"Good," said Jabo. "Real good." He went back for more.

Lila lay against the wall of her little cave. A cushion of moss padded the back of her right shoulder, bruised and sore, which for many nights now kept her from the healing stitches of sleep. Lila closed her eyes and listened: nothing but the loud warble of birds. One confined its range to two or three notes, releasing them in varying time signatures—a kind of ornithological Gregorian chant, Lila thought. Another sang up and down the register, trilling the final note of her run each time, playing games with her practice scales. Still another chirped low and seductive. The woods were full of birds, full of song, performed in achromatic abandon. But the whole, Lila thought, was somehow peaceful. What should have been wild, what might have been merely nature's noise, came together on the breezes in an unsynchronized symphony of passion.

Lila emerged from her cleft of rock to join her daughter on the bank of the creek. Kay Lee rested her head on her mother's shoulder, snuggling close, like a timid pup. Jabo, too, moved closer, experimenting with sending sticks downstream, watching their white-water misadventures from where he stood in a quiet inlet of the creek. Neither one asked after their father.

And they needn't have, for he returned just as Jabo's feet, cold to the point of blue, forced the boy out of the stream to join his sister and mother on the bank.

"Lila, get the baby from that lady friend of yours. Past time we left," J.P. said.

Lila didn't move. Didn't look at him, even.

"You hear me?"

His voice was lower, thicker than usual, the words a syllable or two longer than they should have been. Which meant, she thought, he must have helped himself to the contents of the cooler he'd insisted on tucking away in a corner of the car—just in case. "You can't drive like that," she said, hearing herself as though from a great distance. "Thought you said you were gonna lay off for a while after what happened last time."

"We're leavin'," he said, more loudly than was necessary for the acoustics of the little clearing.

No one moved.

"You kids don't get your butts off that mud in two seconds, I'll give you reason to move."

Lila raised the upper half of her torso to a sitting position but looked at the stream as she spoke. "You needn't bully the children."

"'You needn't,'" he said in a high whine meant to imitate her, "tell me what to do." He took a step closer. Still not looking up, Lila did not need to see the expression on her husband's face to know what was coming. She watched the stream instead.

"Daddy," Kay Lee ventured, "couldn't we stay just a little longer? Momma looks so happy. I hadn't seen her look so—"

"I thought I told you we was leavin'!"

"But, Daddy—"

Lila felt something in the air snap, some great barrier, some clumsily stockaded self-control break loose, and the collapse of that something pulled her to her feet. She turned to face her husband, stepping forward to meet him as his arm swung down towards his daughter. Lila's right shoulder accepted the blow, soundless but for a soft crunch. Her mouth stayed shut, and her eyes closed once, then opened, fixing on her husband's face.

"Daddy, Daddy, please." It was Jabo. Crying. "Daddy, *please.*"

J.P.'s body heaved with the force of an explosion only half complete. Lila waited for his face to turn, as it did at these times, from the puffy red of too many drinks to a purple-gray rage, a face that looked as though it might blow apart at any moment: his thick-bridged nose going one direction, his big, square chin another.

Without shifting focus, eyes fixed on her husband, Lila stepped back. Her hands behind her, she reached towards the bodies of both her children, close beside each other. "Leave," she said to him.

"'Leave,'" he echoed in a high nasal pitch. "The puppies' mother speaks," he gurgled on half-swallowed tobacco juice. His voice's considerable volume was muffled only slightly by the breeze trembling through mountain laurel and stirring the little dogwoods at their tips. "You happy here, puppies' mother? You happy here with these here two slobberin' puppies you spoiled, *you* spoiled into snot-nosed *morons?*"

"Daddy," Jabo sobbed. "Oh, Daddy."

Kay Lee wrapped her arm through her brother's, stroking its downy surface, and pushed her cheek against his. "Hush, Jabby, hush," she whispered.

In one ratchet of his torso, J.P. turned and reached Kay Lee's sneakers protected within the hollow of the chestnut oak. With his passing arm, the one that had made him the high school hero, made Lila Fairbanks the envy of the entire county's sixteen-year-old female population, he sent his daughter's sneakers far, far downstream. "Learned 'em to side with their stinkin', stupid fat cow of a momma, didn't you?"

"Leave," Lila said again.

"I'll kill you, woman. You understand me? I could kill you one-handed." J.P. stepped within reach of his wife, grabbing the collar of her blouse and wrenching her whole body towards him like a yanked dog on a choke chain. His left fist balled itself before her face. "You think I'd married you if I'd knowed how it'd be? You looked at yourself lately? Fat *cow!* Think you're smart, don't you? You like that Lacey woman remindin' you how smart you are. Well I'll tell you somethin' else: you ain't *nothin'* without me. You got nothin' and you ain't nothin'! *You hear me, cow?* Nothin' *without me!"*

"Leave," she said, still holding both children behind her, one under each arm, spread out and back like wings. She closed her eyes.

Hazel Lacey in her Reeboks made a surprising amount of noise for a woman so slight of figure. In one hand she carried the baby, awake now, but quiet, by the handle of his car seat. In the other she swung a brown grocery bag, swung it wildly back and forth like a little girl on a picnic.

"I brought," said Hazel Lacey, "enough Popsicles for everyone, all the grown-up people, that is," she added, setting little Jenks down with a quick-puckered kiss blown after him. From her sack she drew out a banana Popsicle for Kay Lee and one for Jabo and one for Lila and one for herself, then crumpled the empty sack and set it beside her where she dropped herself cross-legged, her dress hiked up above bony white knees, on the bank of the mountain stream.

"I understand," said Hazel Lacey, "that J.P. had to leave." She turned. Reaching out a delicately boned hand to Lila, who was visibly shaking now, she grasped the younger woman's fingers in her own with a strength that was startling in one so old, so little, so frail.

I Had Trouble with Violets

The bib crumpled under her chin like a fan in soiled linen folds as she slumped in her seat, her spine no longer willing to support her flaccid white bulk. But I'd heard about a time when that same spine was not only sturdy but limber, pliant, playful: back when she rode horses and raced children to the lodge at summer camp and taught interpretive dance.

There wasn't much to interpret in her movement now. Her face, her arms, her eyes—their brown depths dammed up, stagnant—told me nothing. I tried to read her face. Maybe she was hungry. Or having trouble swallowing. Maybe by spitting out her dinner, she expected her message to be plainly understood. Strained apricots trickled out the left corner of her mouth. I leaned forward to wipe her chin only to make way for more orange froth. And I thought—and was ashamed of thinking—of the concrete pipe in the woods behind the old stone parsonage back home. From that pipe tumbled a mountain stream, together with the leftover chemicals of a local business upstream—before the town suggested less convenient methods of disposal.

I leaned forward again, this time gagging on the smell of her, the smell of everything around her, the odor of an earthly vessel crumbling back into clay. It didn't seem like a response any caring—any decent—person should have, repulsion at the sight and smell of one's own grandmother. I was ashamed of myself again.

147

"Pardon me, Momay," I said to her and fled to the bathroom. My head dangling low from a convulsing neck, I draped myself onto and over the sink and tried to breathe deeply.

The bathroom, I could see even from that position, had not changed since she'd first moved from the big house in Atlanta, the one with the immaculate, sloping front lawn proudly parading Georgia pines that stood slender and straight, tall enough to tickle the clouds. Here at the assisted-living facility, she'd decorated the bathroom as a kind of memorial to the gardens she'd kept there among the pines on Starlight Drive, a reminder of her years as a young mother when she'd taken turns playing in the rope hammock behind the big house with her three daughters and a son, all blond like her husband and curly headed like her. They would watch spring peek its head in amongst the grass and pine needles in little dapples of lavender and purple and white. It was the violets she loved best. She flooded her bathroom in the retirement home with them: plastic ones and cloth ones and crocheted ones. Violets everywhere.

Her youngest daughter at age eight contracted Rocky Mountain spotted fever from a tick bite at the day camp she'd balked at attending, the one my grandmother insisted would be good for her. That daughter died the year before medical science found a cure. The oldest daughter left the United States to live and work in Japan for the remainder of her life the same week the middle daughter, my mother, married and moved more than 1,000 miles north. But the violets . . . my grandmother kept all the violets with her.

My mother once framed a snapshot taken on an early spring visit to my grandmother in Birmingham, Alabama (hometown to my great-grandmother, grandmother, and mother), in which I, a child of three, had picked violets from the side of the road and was presenting my beloved grandmother's favorite flower to her proudly, ceremoniously, as Gawain might have produced the Grail. The picture was shot beneath the oak tree that stood in what once was my great-grandmother's front yard. Three heads of curly hair blowing in the spring breeze are there beneath the ancient tree: my mother is the smiling spectator, as my grandmother bends over me in an almost greedy solicitude. Four generations, if you count the oak.

As a child, my great-grandmother let her older brothers lower her down a deep well to save a baby pig who'd fallen in. She later defended herself to her mother: it needed to be done, and no one else was willing to do it. In her late teens, she left home to teach children in Appalachia for something like the same reasons. As an adult, she played a mean game of tennis and mastered the violin and opened a tea room and sold real estate for fun. She wore a corset to the day she died. I don't believe my great-grandmother would have minded an oak tree as a stand-in.

I always loved that photograph taken on my great-grandmother's front yard. It said something powerful to me as a child about what it was to be female—and in particular, what it was to be female in my family. Violets and oaks, I understood that picture to explain, are what you come from. Violets and oaks have given something of their lives to give you strength as well as grace.

But just then, somehow, still heaving over the sink in my grandmother's violet-heavy bathroom, I had no genuine sense of relatedness to her, no comfort in being part of a chain of life, no awareness of the female strength and wisdom that she had passed on

to me. I was conscious at that moment of her being my mother's mother only because old photographs on the walls and keepsakes on the shelves and the nameplate on the nursing-home-room door testified that it was so. I saw nothing of myself—nothing I wanted to see, at least—in the slumping body beneath a soiled linen bib; a head crowned with white curls smashed flat against the face; toes, twisted and blue, peeking out from beneath an afghan.

And too, there was the fact that as a young woman in my first year of graduate school—and, belatedly, my first year of "finding myself"—I wasn't at all sure I liked what those violets represented. To me they spoke of quiet, unassuming sweetness, easily trampled without the slightest notice, often overlooked, rarely prized for anything other than pretty simplicity. I was part of a generation taught to prize the "goodies" so long withheld from women: power and influence and professional notice. The oak I could be proud of, hope to emulate even. But I had trouble with violets.

Washing my mouth out, I returned to the woman's side and knelt to cover her bare feet because objective testimony told me this was my mother's mother, and some primal sense of duty insisted I must. Her feet, like her toes, lay in contorted crescents, rough flesh over gnarled bones like the protruding roots of an old chestnut. There had been a time when my grandmother's flesh had been a friend to her. Her face stayed supple and unnoticeably lined, well into old age, even after I was ruining my own skin in summers spent outdoors in and around and on water—and sun. But her flesh was failing her now.

My grandmother's ankles swelled over her feet in tumid balloons, taut and purplish blue. I sat marveling that these same feet once fit into toe shoes, these same ankles were once bound with pink satin ribbon, this same body stood supported on two such feet, such ankles—and executed flawless *assemblés*.

Soon after I'd begun breaking in my own first pair of toe shoes, someone gave me a painting of a ballerina re-lacing the ribbons at her ankles before a performance. My grandmother joined me in admiring it, but she was quick to point out the dancer's legs. "See the thighs? Too heavy," she said. "That woman could never stay up on her toes." A stranger might have found it a peculiar comment coming from a woman carrying, at that time, more than twice her

ideal weight. But those who knew her before Parkinson's and other debilitating diseases took first her motor and then her verbal skills and finally her sparkle—those who knew her history, knew her *spirit,* had little trouble thinking of her as a dancer still.

Yesterday was my grandmother's birthday—or would have been had she lived to celebrate it. The day she died, I was nearly 3,000 miles away. The possessor of nonrefundable tickets, I was about to travel 3,000 miles yet farther away (a delayed honeymoon trip from a generous relative) from the memorial service in Atlanta. We'd thought the end might come when it did; we'd talked about it ahead of time. "She wouldn't want you to come back for this," my mother insisted again over the phone. "She'd be the first to tell you and Todd to go ahead and have a lovely honeymoon."

So while I was sitting in a cabana eating banana-macadamia nut pancakes by the pool at Napili Shores, my family gathered and told stories of my grandmother's life, remembering her many sacrifices for them and singing all her favorite hymns.

No doubt my mother was right about my grandmother. She would have demanded that I not be there, would have pointed out that, since her body was promised to Emory University for medical research and her spirit expected elsewhere, she would be technically absent from the event herself. And my mother was insistent that I not go to Atlanta for her sake. The most forgiving and utterly unself-pitying creature I've ever known, my mother has probably never once looked back to resent that her daughter was not there to help pack away the last of her mother's violets. My mother has much of the oak in her.

Still, as I move through the years, I become increasingly aware of the importance of the simple *being there* of life, being present for those landmark events: the graduations and the promotions and the weddings, the births and the surgeries . . . and the deaths. Being there is a gift to others, a gift to ourselves. It probably was the best decision at the time, missing the memorial service and not the honeymoon. Still, I've noticed the loss.

Yesterday, on my grandmother's birthday, I tried to remember old family stories about her at her best. Instead, I was haunted by the recollection of my last visit with her, of apricot drool trickling from ineffectual, quivering lips. It distressed me that, of everything noble and lovely about her, this was what my mind's scrapbook turned to now: apricot drool.

Maybe that final image disturbed me not only because it represented her complete helplessness at the end but also because it represented a partial helplessness with which she lived, often painfully, though always gracefully: believing at the time that she was living the way she should, the way others expected. At the end of her life, she wished she'd suppressed a little less, spoken up a little more. For the good of others, as well as herself. The violets, I think, were sometimes crushed.

In her girlhood, my grandmother wrote poetry and painted and memorized Shakespeare and danced. As a young woman, she raised her children to love the arts and read widely, to seek truth and pursue advanced degrees. In middle age, she nurtured juvenile offenders and poured tea for wealthy Southern lady friends, who chided her for what they called her liberal treatment of the "colored help."

But yesterday morning on my grandmother's

birthday, all I could recall were the paintings never hung in prestigious galleries, the poetry never published, the dancing career never played out, the societal-reform work never given professional status, the angry, honest, needful words never uttered—for the sake of four children, for the sake of a hot-tempered husband, for the sake of family harmony. Yesterday, on my grandmother's birthday, I remembered a life that seemed to me tragically without the fanfare, without the recognition, it should have earned.

Today I was still thinking of my grandmother as I sat at the computer playing with words on the screen—edgy and frustrated with not finding just the right words. Yet still, strangely, doing the only thing I wanted to be doing. And for the first time in many years, I remembered the hours and hours of Scrabble with my grandmother, played on the front porch of her cabin in the mountains of North Carolina. Early in the morning, the pine needles on the porch still damp, the wood stove in the old kitchen just kindled, we would sit with hot chocolate warming our hands and sort letters in endless configurations on a green vinyl tablecloth, always searching for the Right Words. This, I learned from my grandmother, was important work, worthy of rising early.

Today I heard my husband carrying our daughter down the stairs, stopping halfway and asking the ritual question: "Julia, where is the prettiest painting in the whole world?" I knew, without seeing, she was pointing to the watercolor hanging above the staircase. "Good girl," I heard him say, "and who painted it?" "Momma," she completed the liturgy, and the two of them proceeded down the stairs for the next ritual of the day: her Cheerios, his coffee.

The watercolor is, of course, not only *not* the prettiest painting in the world but not even *good* by any objective standard that excludes the critique of close relations. But today I remembered for the first time in years that my grandmother bought me my first set of oil paints and brushes and three little canvases, then showed me her own work and praised mine. Putting one's own view of the world into paint, she taught me, is a way of sharing beauty.

Today I prepared to teach an English class. And for the first time in years, I heard my grandmother's voice reciting poetry: classics she'd memorized in her teen years at Agnes Scott before the Depression took the private college out of her reach, and then at the University of Alabama. Even after her mind had begun to blur facts and figures and grandchildren's names, my mother's mother could recite Shakespeare. Great literature, I learned from her, is a treasure worth locking in your mind.

Today I played with my daughter on the livingroom floor and watched her, unprompted by me, begin to dance. Tchaikovsky, Vince Gill, Bob Dylan . . . it matters little: she simply loves to dance. My grandmother, I remembered today, came up from Atlanta to see my last dance recital, my class performing a portion of Swan Lake. How proud I was for her to see us in our white net-and-feather splendor. How awkward we must have been, we swans. But if my grandmother saw that, she also must have seen something else: we all just loved to dance.

Today I fed my dog and secured the fence to keep her out of the street, a country lane turned shortcut by hurried commuters. And I remembered my first dog, my only other dog, who grew up on another busy street far away. Though I never should have had a dog on such a busy street, my father sympathized with my unreasoning passion for animals. And my grandmother, seeing how terribly shy I was, agreed, convinced my mother I desperately needed a dog—and paid for the fence.

That puppy, whom my father helped me pick out on my thirteenth birthday, was my closest friend for years. She died within a week of my grandmother, the week of my honeymoon.

My grandmother would have loved the man I married. But today I remembered that she liked another man I almost married, liked him a lot. And I realized how sad, how strangely predictable, that was. He reminded her, she told me once, of her own husband. They had some things in common: two charming Southern gentlemen, two volcanic tempers.

In my own case, I ignored—and will never know why I did—too many balled-up fists in my face, too many times of being jerked by my coat collar across a car seat, too many times of being called stupid. And to have tolerated his tantrums, I was indeed being extraordinarily stupid, though that was not at all what he meant, of course.

Thanks be to God for shattering moments of clarity, lightning flashes in the rumbling dark. It was when I first turned my back on him to walk away in rage, the time he grabbed me by the hair and yanked me back to him, that I was finally able to walk away for good.

My grandmother wept when my mother told her of the broken engagement. I don't know if she made connections between the two men's tempers as she'd done with their charm: I don't know if my drawing those connections was fair to my grandfather. I do know I once hurt my grandmother by letting her overhear me make the comparison between the two men in attempting to explain the broken engagement to an aunt. Certainly, I was insensitive, and I may have been wrong as well.

In any case, I know that whatever my grandmother endured during the early and middle years of her marriage, she did live to see her husband change. *Repentance,* I suppose, is the only fitting description—and my grandmother always did insist upon the right word. In many ways he had always been a good man; but from all accounts, he was an altogether better man during the final years of his life. My grandmother lived to enjoy, at least at the end, the marriage she'd meant to have in the first place.

And she lived to see her only granddaughter marry a man she herself would have adored, had her mind been clear enough then to know him well. Even through the haze of disease, she knew enough, I believe, to applaud my choice. It was through her I learned to be grateful for the lessons learned early, as well as the lessons learned at last.

Today I watch my daughter go bounding, tireless, down the hill of our backyard to the town forest (she so loves the woods), and I wonder if she will be a dancer or a painter or a writer or a teacher or a social reformer—or maybe a forest ranger. It is May, the day after my grandmother's birthday, and here in New England little splashes of lavender and purple and white are just beginning to appear among grass that is trying to return to green.

I scoop my daughter in my arms, wriggling (she wants to stay outside), and in the kitchen pour her apple juice in a tippy cup and myself hot tea in a cup left me by my grandmother, an English bone-china cup with violets on it. And my daughter and I drink to the intricate, mysterious chain of life, and to one particular life which today I honor.

Dorilee Davis Saw Death

Dorilee Davis first saw death hanging by a rope in her twelve-year-old boy's bedroom closet.

Death, in any shape or form, she told Jarvis later, had never been part of the plan when, at seventeen, Dorilee had strategically mapped her escape out of Sequatchie County, Tennessee. She launched her personal campaign for happiness in life by marrying the hometown celebrity, Bud Davis, an All-American quarterback with a blond crew cut and a koala-bear face and big mop-bucketfuls of college scholarship offers.

Nor was death particularly on her mind when at nineteen she worked nights changing geriatric-ward bedpans at Piedmont Community Hospital while the sweet-faced husband stumbled over Cicero and shuffled through Shakespeare and finally accepted a diploma purchased for him by the head football coach, Jake Cotter—who apparently knew the young man's value better than some short-sighted literature professors. Bud's junior-year thesis began, "F. Scott Fitzgerald was a very good writer, but he drank too much when he was still real young" (which also summed up the remaining twenty pages of the paper). After Jake Cotter helpfully pointed out its stronger points to the academic dean, the thesis earned a C-: just enough, as it happened, to keep Bud Davis off academic probation.

"I should have gone to college," Dorilee Davis would say years later, not to anyone in particular.

But Jarvis Darby, the girl from down the street who fed the cat and raked the yard, was sometimes standing nearby. On those occasions when Jarvis was present, Dorilee might pivot her wheelchair with one flip of a finger back towards the girl and repeat herself, louder this time: "I should have gone to college."

"Yes, ma'am," Jarvis would say, because there was nothing else to say. There it was, and not much anyone could do about it now.

Jarvis had been hired from among the neighborhood youths because she spoke little, worked hard, and was far too much a loner to have many friends eager for the gossip that anyone working for Dorilee Davis might have provided. Jarvis Darby had been chosen because she could hold her tongue, but there were days when the girl's simple "yes, ma'am" fell far short of what Dorilee needed to hear.

Death in any shape or form had not been part of her plan when she was seventeen, Dorilee explained to Jarvis later. "Even hauling away bedpans for a living from under immobile ninety-eight-year-olds," she said, "you'd be surprised how little a nineteen-year-old's life has anything to do with death."

And anything but death figured into the long-range vision of a twenty-one-year-old Dorilee Davis when she learned to play tennis, once their financial position allowed—even insisted upon—membership in the local club. Outside sports, Bud was basically shy and left most of the socializing to his pretty young wife. By the time Dorilee turned twenty-eight, the *Mount Airy Dispatch* sports section was giving quarter pages to pictures of her: always tanned and slender and graceful, always laughing and evidently saying something awfully clever to one of her regular string of tournament partners: always tanned and slender and graceful—typically male and typically not her husband.

Jarvis could not remember those days herself; that was well before she was born. But Dorilee once showed her clippings in a scrapbook. Not, of course, that Jarvis didn't already know about the sports-page photos before she'd ever met her down-the-street neighbor, since those photos were part of the story people told about Dorilee. In a small town, folks know things about other folks they don't actually know.

Jarvis was sitting on the back porch swing when Dorilee wheeled up to her and spread the scrapbook on the girl's lap. "If you're going to be feeding my cat, you need to see this," Dorilee had said. Jarvis flipped pages obediently but said nothing. Now and then she looked up to see Dorilee staring at her, as though waiting for a judgment.

Bud Davis brought his wife iced tea just then and frowned, not exactly at Jarvis—his koala face was incapable of frowning *at* anyone—but certainly in the direction of the scrapbook. "They liked her," he defended his wife to Jarvis, who had yet to speak, "because she was good. There was people who couldn't understand that. They liked her because she was good."

Accepting the iced tea with her one good hand, Dorilee Davis looked her husband in the face without comment. *"Were,"* she said at last. "There *were* people who couldn't understand." Then she turned to Jarvis. "The corner of the yard by the weeping cherry hasn't been raked."

When Jarvis got home that afternoon, she mentioned the scrapbook to her mother, then wished she hadn't.

"What did that woman mean showing those newspaper pictures to an impressionable young girl? And I suppose she didn't bother to show you the other clippings, Jarvis?"

"Other clippings?"

"The ones about her boy, Danny. You know about that, Jarvis."

"No, ma'am."

"Of course you do. You remember your father and I were concerned about that whole thing—told you all about it—when Mrs. Davis first asked you to work for her."

"I mean 'no, ma'am,' she didn't show me."

"Not surprising she wouldn't finish the story for you. You don't forget the end of the story now, you hear?"

"Yes, ma'am."

In all the years Jarvis raked the yard and fed the cat, Dorilee Davis never mentioned the other clippings, the ones about her boy, Danny. Never specifically anyway. Naturally, Jarvis knew the story. Everyone did: how Dorilee Davis, nearly thirty, found death hanging by a rope in Danny's closet.

At the time, the papers said it wasn't clear whether the twelve-year-old boy had committed suicide—as everyone knows adolescents sometimes do—or whether the hanging was the accidental outcome of playing around with rope in the absence of responsible adult supervision. The papers didn't spell it out exactly, but everyone in town who knew—or knew about—Dorilee Davis could read between the lines: either way, the whole messy incident had something to do with a married woman's spending way too much time on the tennis courts with other people's husbands.

"My son, Danny, had red hair, you know," Dorilee once told Jarvis as the girl raked, under supervision from the wheelchair that followed her around the yard.

"Red." Jarvis had nodded, hoping that would be sufficient.

"Neither of us do, you know. Neither Bud nor I."

Jarvis nodded again.

"Danny wet his bed sometimes, even at twelve."

Jarvis raked faster. "I reckon that happens sometimes."

"They say it can be a sign of distress, bed-wetting. Anyone ever told you that?"

Jarvis shook her head.

Dorilee flipped her chair into reverse. "They've told me that often enough."

Jarvis Darby knew Dorilee's story, had known it for years in the same way she knew that the drugstore on the corner of Ridgeway and Fairmont had a low candy counter and an aging pharmacist whose bifocals needed a new prescription. It was a town in which certain personal information was understood to be in the public domain. Jarvis's involvement with Dorilee Davis herself, though, began long after the death of Dorilee's only child, who hung himself—accidentally or not—in his bedroom closet, and long after Dorilee and her husband let their country club memberships expire.

If pressed, Jarvis could have traced her own first recollections of Dorilee Davis as a town personage of a certain fame to one summer afternoon when Jarvis was playing at Arlene Veal's house. Arlene's mother, Jolene, who worked at the Mount Airy Country Club, came home saying the Davises weren't keeping up with their monthly membership dues. Country clubs were not, after all, charity boards, she said. The membership would simply have to be terminated.

The two little girls were playing with Arlene's Barbie in the shrubbery by the sidewalk. Arlene looked up and asked, "How come, Momma?"

"Because, dear, even All-Americans learn at middle age they can't always pay the mortgage on the past, glory days or not. And I believe it would be fair to say the Davises have lost their taste for socializing. Remind me to tell ya'll the whole sordid story someday when you're old enough."

Intrigued, Jarvis and Arlene made up their own version of the story that day and let Barbie act it out. But they weren't sure how to end it, so just before dinner they let Arlene's dog run off with Barbie in his mouth.

Later, Jarvis understood what she could not yet grasp that summer afternoon—that the Davises were doing the only thing they could do: guarding their private lives with the ferocity a small town requires from the shy and the tragic.

Jarvis's father, a deacon at the Baptist church, once participated in a carefully strategized mission to the Davises' house. The Methodists and the Presbyterians had made their own previous attempts at Dorilee's redemption. Some people even said the Episcopalians had discussed an attempt at outreach, given the extenuating circumstances, though no one ever confirmed the rumor. The Baptists weren't surprised those who'd gone before had failed, but they were less well prepared for their own reception at the hands of Dorilee Davis.

"Didn't so much as ask us to sit," Jarvis Darby's father told her mother. "Fresh-baked pecan pie sitting right there on the coffee table, but she didn't offer a one of us any. Not so much as a glass of iced tea."

"Might just as well slammed the door in your face."

So Bud and Dorilee kept to themselves. And Jarvis Darby never would have known Dorilee Davis, not personally anyway, if Jarvis hadn't been sick a whole lot in third grade. As it was that year, she used to have nightmares about Dorilee Davis as a stampeding white monster with bared teeth, chasing small children with vials of blood and razor blades and glass beakers.

Dorilee Davis at middle age was a nurse's aide at the pediatrician's office. Nearly all the children feared her, and those who didn't fear her, despised her. She always smelled of stale tobacco and rubbing alcohol—and often, too, as Jarvis's mother pointed out to the pediatrician, "of alcohol not for external use only, Doctor, if you know what I mean. You really should do something about that woman."

When Dorilee Davis drew blood from her young victims, she made them look up into the glare of the fluorescent ceiling light until they quit wriggling. "Hold still. Hold *still,*" Dorilee would say, breathing hard-grain alcohol fumes into terror-stricken little faces.

Dorilee Davis, in fact, was the reason Jarvis never would go frog-gigging summer nights at the Blue Hole with her brother and Freddy Hawkins. Figured she knew what the frogs felt like staring up into the flashlight, mesmerized, just waiting to be harpooned.

It was during the period she worked at the pediatrician's office that Dorilee met up with death for the second time. Immoderate doses of tobacco and alcohol (not of the rubbing variety) and tragedy eventually took their toll on Dorilee Davis's health.

The stroke she suffered at fifty-seven permanently immobilized her entire right side.

"My doctor," Dorilee later told Jarvis as the two of them planted petunias, one digging and adjusting and watering, the other supervising, "my doctor washed his hands of me that day. Marched into my hospital room and said he'd done everything he knew to warn me. He'd begged me to make changes, in diet, in lifestyle, prescribed pills, tried to help. He could do nothing more; he'd given up, he said."

"Yes, ma'am."

"Don't be too quick to judge, Jarvis. He was right about me, you know. Had every right to give up on me. Said he was a busy man with other patients who both needed him *and* would listen to his counsel. Said I could either seek help elsewhere or lie there and ferment or go straight to hell with his blessings—but he wasn't sticking around to watch."

Jarvis looked up from her leaves. "He said that?"

"He had a point, you know, but he had a face like a ferret."

Immediately after the stroke, Dorilee had recognized her need for help around the house and yard.

She hired a cleaning woman and a yard man, but three years later, little things were still slipping through the cracks, getting left undone. And then, too, Dorilee Davis had to admit she wished for someone to just be . . . around. So Dorilee asked the quiet little girl down the street if she wanted to make a little spending money doing odd jobs.

"Start saving now," Jarvis's father had told her. "Age twelve is not too young to start looking at the future. If you want to be the first in the family to go to college, you'd better be doing something more than wishing." So in sixth grade Jarvis began feeding Dorilee's cat—and with effort, overcame her horror of the stampeding white monster nurse with bared teeth.

That was how, at age twelve, Jarvis Darby learned to recognize the Davises' car when Dorilee drove past the elementary school in the morning during Mrs. Buckshorn's social studies class. (With help getting in and out, Dorilee could, with one hand and one foot, operate a car on the quieter roads of the town.) And then in the afternoons, Dorilee would come poking back the other way, often just as recess began and the children came spilling out into the field, snatching up the jump ropes and the balls as they ran, shedding jackets and scarves in heaps around the parallel bars.

A few of the sixth-grade girls always trickled back into the woods, daily rearranging the bits of broken glass and hickory nuts and moss-backed boulders in the clearing that housed imaginary—but nonetheless elaborate—pioneer cabins and teepees and a home base for Nancy Drew, girl detective. But the woods sat on the side of the field bordered by Fairmont Road, where Dorilee came driving by at recess. And sometimes her old white Chevy would sit there for a while, the engine running, not going anywhere.

"Gives me the creeps," Arlene Veal complained almost daily. "Just because the old witch lets you feed her cat, Jarvis, doesn't mean she gets to follow you around."

Some of the boys playing kick ball on the playground learned to recognize Dorilee's car too. Seeing it, they would run snatch the jump rope away from a cluster of girls in the middle of chanting, "Cinderella, dressed in yella, went upstairs to kiss a fella. . . ."

"Hide the rope!" the boys would shout. "It's old-lady Davis! Hide the rope!" Everyone knew about Dorilee's boy, Danny, and the closet. The jump rope was too tempting a taunt.

Arlene Veal did her part by making faces in the direction of Dorilee Davis. Arlene could make the best, the scariest, faces of anyone, partly because she was the meanest of the sixth-grade girls (though she never would join in when others made fun of Jarvis's clothes, well broken in by two older brothers). But also, there was Arlene's nose. Two years before, when she was out riding, her saddle slid (she never would check the girth but once) clear around to the horse's belly, swinging her, and her nose, into the ground. By way of a fence post. Arlene's parents never had the money to fix the nose right, so she lived with it jagged, looking like a bolt of lightning down her face. In sixth grade, the things Arlene Veal did with her face were perfectly amazing.

Rusty Cotter, oldest son of Jake, the head football coach, sometimes ran with the other boys who snatched the jump rope and shouted things to Dorilee Davis as she drove by, but he had trouble keeping up. He was always the first one out in dodge ball (even before the girls) and the last one down in the spelling bees (even after the girls), so everyone wondered about him. Once, he tried joining the girls during recess at the fringe of the woods, but they laughed at him for thinking any boy could be Indian princess Running Deer or Nancy Drew.

In kick ball, Rusty never slid to the bases as the other boys did, so his blue jeans stayed dark blue and stiff and all in one piece. Sitting right beside him in Mrs. Buckshorn's class, Jarvis Darby caught him one day taking scissors to the knees of his pants, cutting out perfect, round holes, as though he'd punched through the fabric with a cookie cutter.

"Whatcha doing?" Jarvis asked, fingering her own jeans, barely still connected at the knees after two older brothers.

"Don't tell anybody. Please?" Rusty asked, blinking hard. "Please don't tell anybody."

She never did. Not, at least, anybody Rusty would have meant by "anybody."

Jarvis did tell Dorilee Davis months later when Dorilee asked about that boy in the sixth-grade class who was so much smaller than the others.

"You mean to tell me the boy with the porthole knees is Jake Cotter's son? I never, never in a million years, would have guessed it."

"Coach Cotter's younger boy, Zeb—he's in fifth grade—looks more like his daddy."

"You say Rusty is good in school, Jarvis?"

"He does real good."

"Real *well.*"

"Either way, makes it hard on his daddy."

"Is that what people say?"

"I reckon. Yes, ma'am."

"People say his dad's not . . . encouraging of him?"

"Don't come right out and say it, I don't reckon. But Rusty's daddy brags a lot about Zeb, says Zeb's got a real chance of making something of himself."

From the time Jarvis caught Rusty Cotter with the scissors, he wore those deep navy jeans with perfectly round kneecap-sized holes in them. It took months for the holes to begin to fray at the edges. But as Arlene Veal enjoyed pointing out, no one ever told him not to button a flannel shirt up to the very top button, so you could still pick him out of the crowd as the A+ nerd.

Jarvis Darby went on raking the Davises' yard and feeding the cat, sometimes taking out the trash and watering the lawn and rearranging the deck furniture. From sixth grade all the way through high school, her duties expanded over the years, along with the time she spent shadowed by or following after or working beside the wheelchair from which Dorilee Davis held court.

"Jarvis, you must've missed watering the petunias last week. They've looked sick and dizzy these past five days."

"Yes, ma'am."

"And you missed the trash can in the guest room last week."

"Yes, ma'am."

"Jarvis?"

"Yes, ma'am?"

"Do I pay you enough to put up with me?"

"Arlene Veal thinks you pay me way too much."

"Ah. And who, pray tell, is Arlene Veal?"

"A friend. My age."

"More specific."

"She used to yell at you when we were younger and you'd drive by the elementary school playground."

"More specific. You've yet to narrow it."

"Her nose—"

"*That's* Arlene Veal! What on earth happened to that child's face?"

"She broke it on a horse. We were out riding."

"Well, she looks a fright. Somebody ought to make her fix it."

"I don't know if the Veals' insurance covered cosmetic surgery."

"I don't know if I'd call dragging a nose back so it sits somewhere in the ballpark of between two eyes cosmetic. You can tell your friend Arlene I asked about her—and her nose—if you like."

Jarvis would just as soon not have mentioned the conversation—ever—to Arlene, but Dorilee Davis clearly meant the permission she gave as a command.

"What's the old hag want with me and my nose?" Arlene said cheerfully, having resigned herself years ago to the lightning bolt down the center of her face. At least she had a good voice, she knew: she spoke often of going into radio.

"Don't know. She just asked. Dorilee just asks things sometimes."

"You know, Jarvis, people say she was a knockout when she was younger. My mom said all the men were nuts for her, that even—"

"She was. I saw pictures once. I don't know about the . . . men . . . being nuts. . . ."

"You wouldn't ever guess it to look at the old crone now, would you?"

Jarvis shrugged, and Arlene, for once, respected the cue to change the subject. But all that Saturday afternoon watering the lawn, Jarvis looked at Dorilee Davis out of the corner of her eye. Arlene was right. Roman ruins at least suggested to a vivid imagination that beauty and grace once stood there. Not so with Dorilee Davis. Jarvis had seen the old sports-page clippings, had seen the hard evidence. Still, she found it hard to picture Dorilee Davis as anything but what she was now, the victim of a stroke that immobilized half her face, preventing her from smiling. Jarvis had seen Dorilee slip a time or two in the past couple of years, slip and almost smile, but the effect of half a mouth turned up and half remaining limp was pathetic. Dorilee knew it and never could permit it of herself.

Dorilee called Jarvis over to her at the end of the

day. "You want to tell me what you're thinking?"

"No, ma'am. Not particularly."

"Okay. I can understand that. Tell me anyway."

"People talk about how you looked when you were younger."

"Ravishing. Is that what they say? Yes? Well, it's good to know they keep the gossip in this town accurate and up-to-date. There now. That settled, tell me, Jarvis, how is that Cotter boy? Rusty."

"Smart as ever. But trips over seams in the sidewalk."

"Is he playing any sports?"

"His daddy saw to it he got put on every team the high school's got."

"But he never gets to play?"

"He does good in chess."

"*Well*. Does *well*. Listen . . . , Jarvis?"

"Yes, ma'am?"

"You told me your innermost thoughts; I'm going to tell you mine."

"You don't have to." Confidences always made Jarvis nervous. And coming from Dorilee Davis, you never knew what you might get.

"Today, Jarvis, I have been missing my son."

"Danny?"

"Danny. My baby. I miss him every day, you understand. Just some days are tougher than others."

"This is one of the tougher days?"

"This is one of the tougher days."

Jarvis went and sat beside the wheelchair then, and stayed there, saying nothing, as the two of them watched the leaf pile Jarvis had just raked dance back across the lawn into that day's first position. Neither of them spoke or moved until Bud came to the door to call them in. The Dolphins were playing the Cowboys. "Thought we might all watch it together," he said, "since the chili and cheese grits on the stove is going bad if nobody eats it."

Dorilee squeezed his arm with her good hand as she motored by him. "*Are*," she said. "*Are* going bad."

So Jarvis Darby spent most Saturday afternoons from the time she was twelve to the time she was seventeen at Dorilee Davis's house. At seventeen, she went away to college, the tuition paid for with money she'd saved over the years feeding the cat and raking the leaves and taking out the trash. All her worldly goods packed in a powder blue Pinto with 106,000 miles on it, Jarvis left for school, stopping by Dorilee's on her way out of town.

Whirring back away from the front door in a perfectly executed leftward sweep of her wheelchair, Dorilee fetched a package from the coffee table. "I thought you might need this for college," she said, watching, her eyebrows bunched together, as Jarvis pulled from the box a pink monogrammed sweater, a matching blouse, and a gray wool skirt.

Jarvis' breath snagged somewhere in the back of her throat. Rather than speak, she held the sweater to her chest tentatively and then, more boldly, the skirt to her waist.

"The skirt's handmade," Dorilee told her brusquely.

"*You* . . . ?"

"I still have one side operational, remember."

"But . . ."

"It was good exercise."

"I *love* pink."

"I know."

"You do?"

"You've worn pink bandanas for years with work shirts that didn't match. I figured there had to be a reason. There's not enough pink walking around out there in this world anyway. So there you are."

"It's just so . . . beautiful. And you're so . . ." Jarvis never found the right word, but Dorilee Davis seemed to hear it anyway. She very nearly smiled.

Jarvis Darby came home from college once a semester or so and always dropped by Dorilee Davis's to see if the leaves needed raking or the cat needed feeding. Freddy Hawkins was taking care of all that now in his spare time from the fishing-supply business. But Jarvis dropped by just the same—just in case someone had missed watering the petunias—and stayed to talk.

"Jarvis?" Dorilee said on one of these visits.

"Yes, ma'am?"

"Push me closer by the fire, dear. And while you're near me, let me tell you something I've been wanting you to know."

Jarvis braced herself, praying that Bud Davis, who was humming to himself as he washed the dinner dishes, wouldn't join them anytime soon, just in case Dorilee had gotten it into her head to talk about the past. "Yes, ma'am?" Jarvis bent over the wheelchair.

"You know a thing or two about me, Jarvis."

"Yes, ma'am."

"And probably could guess at more. You're a smart girl. You know I've gotten a good look at death a time or two."

"Yes, ma'am."

"I want you to remember this: there's more than one kind of death."

Jarvis nodded.

"There's the kind when you quit breathing and the kind when you quit caring if you're breathing. You make sure you know the difference."

Jarvis nodded again and was still there, still silent, when Bud reentered the room with hot chocolate for the three of them in two ceramic mugs and one spill-proof cup. As he bent down beside his wife, reaching across her wheelchair to place the cup gently in her one good hand, Dorilee turned her head to kiss the inside of his arm. The two of them froze there for a time, something passing between them that Jarvis could feel as surely as if it had gently but firmly pushed her aside. She studied the patterns in the throw rug at her feet.

In the spring of her junior year, Jarvis came home from college to serve punch at the fiftieth wedding-anniversary party of Bud and Dorilee Davis.

When she'd first called to tell Jarvis about it the winter before, Dorilee had sounded as surprised by her own plans as anyone. "But you know," she reasoned over the phone, "there are just a few more things this old flesh has yet to see." Jarvis waited for more. "Then, too, Bud and I haven't seen half the town since . . ." That was as far as Dorilee got.

"For a long, long time," Jarvis filled in then, and accepted the honor of serving at the party.

The anniversary-party punch had become a great green mushroom cloud of froth when Jarvis added more ginger ale to the lime sherbet, a foamy head now edging far over the bowl's sterling-silver sides. She was still trying to get the hang of ladling out something besides foam into guests' cups when someone touched her on the shoulder.

"I like your sweater" was the first thing Arlene Veal said, holding out her cup and grinning. "Monogrammed, too. Very classy. You look nice in pink, Jarvis. I hadn't remembered that."

"Arlene Veal . . . your nose! . . ." Jarvis dropped the ladle.

"Whatcha think of it? Better? Lost something of its character, I fear—not so easy to describe me to strangers anymore."

"It's . . . straight!"

"And small too, don't you think? I requested Audrey Hepburn, but they said I didn't have the cheekbones for it. Came as close as they could."

"But how . . . ?"

"That's enough about me. Except to tell you—get this—I'm the anchorwoman for the university's news program. Television! Can you believe it? Me! You know I always wanted to do TV, but there was always—"

"There was always your *nose*. All those faces you could make!"

"Yeah, well, that's the tragic part: I had to give up the faces. If we were still playing Indians in the playground woods, old Face of a Thousand Corners would have to change her name. But tell me how you've been. . . ."

They covered the first round of preliminary catching up when Jarvis spotted another old friend across the hall. "Look, Arly. Over there."

"Well, darn my socks. It's little Rusty Cotter. Little Rusty Cotter tripping over the table leg. How refreshing. Some things never change. I couldn't have told you Rusty Cotter even knew Dorilee Davis—more than knew about her, I mean. Did you know they were friends, Jarvis?"

Jarvis shrugged and toyed with the punch ladle and, looking down at the froth, she said, "I just fed the cat."

Arlene Veal watched Jarvis's face for a moment. "Mm-hmm. And my nose fixed itself one night under a full moon. C'mon, kid. Let's go see old Naked Knees."

Jarvis left her position of honor at the punch table long enough to join Arlene in greeting Rusty, who was sitting close beside Dorilee Davis.

"Princeton is unquestionably everything I'd hoped it would be," he was telling Dorilee as the young women approached. "Vastly superior, in fact, to my most fantastic imaginings."

Dorilee almost smiled but caught herself, not willing to risk looking pathetic. "Two more questions and then you're through. One, are Yankees as rude as everyone says? And two, are you set, you know, for the rest of the term?"

Rusty Cotter had time, barely, to answer both questions affirmatively, laughing and taking Dorilee's one good hand before Arlene descended upon him, Jarvis standing behind her with a shy wave.

Freddy Hawkins and his kids were there too, Jarvis noticed. As usual, the kids were out of control—just as they'd been ever since Freddy's wife left him three years ago (went out for eggs and never came back). Donna had gotten pregnant when Freddy was still of a frog-gigging age—fourteen or so, as best Jarvis could recall. Freddy and Donna got married because that's just what you did in their town when those kinds of things came up. But, then too . . . sometimes later somebody went out for eggs and never come back.

The Hawkins kids were running a slalom course between guests' legs. Tumbling over one another, they toppled into, under, and across an already heaving dessert table. Through the parlor and down the hall they raced, chasing their dog, Cherries Jubilee on his paws. But this was the first time in quite a while Jarvis had seen the kids not looking like half-starved mongrels, eating off plates that other people had left on chairs and coffee tables.

That was something anyhow. And though slathered now in Cherries Jubilee, they looked as though, several layers down, they might have been clean at the start of the day.

All through the fiftieth wedding celebration, Dorilee's husband, with his gray crew cut and his koala-bear face, stood beside his wife's wheelchair and stroked her hair, stopping only to turn another page in the wedding album. He let his other hand rest on the shoulder of Dorilee's good side, where she could reach up to stroke her husband's fingers when she needed to.

Now and then between guests in the reception line, Dorilee would manage to catch Jarvis's eye. Sometimes she would wink (her one good eye) and twice she mouthed, *Thank you*. Once, she wheeled over to Jarvis's table, saying only, "They tell me I'm as ravishing as ever."

Jarvis wiped smeared lipstick from the side of Dorilee's face that the stroke had left without feeling. "Yes, ma'am," she said. And they both laughed.

Bud Davis didn't say much that day. He rarely did. Even in their country-club days, Bud, unlike Dorilee, had never been one for the art of conversation. Over the past years, his social skills had rusted to uselessness, but he had a way of smiling at his guests, his big, round brown eyes spilling out big, round tears anytime anyone said something touching, so that everyone went away feeling as though they'd had a good, long talk with him.

Jarvis felt privileged when, needing a break from greeting guests, Bud Davis ducked over to the punch table. "She should've been the one to go to college . . . ," he began, faltering.

Jarvis offered him a cup of punch, for something to do with his hands, which were visibly shaking from the strain of greeting so many people only vaguely familiar. "College was a waste on me. Thank you for doing this—the punch—today. Means a whole lot, your being here—to her especially. You'll never know."

"It's a lovely party. So many people."

"I didn't know we knew this many people. Anymore, I mean. You know. There for a while people weren't so eager to keep company. . . . Or maybe it was us ran 'em off. After, you know . . . after Danny. After our boy . . . ." Bud Davis's big, round brown eyes asked for help.

Jarvis refilled his punch cup. "Lots of people here now."

Bud Davis brightened then. "Yeah. Now. If only I didn't have to think of something to say to all jillion of them. Rather let Dorilee do the talking. She's always been good at that."

But Bud was the one who did the talking the day after Dorilee saw death for the third time. He reached Jarvis by phone that very morning, just as she was walking out the door of her dorm room to her eight o'clock class. By noon, Jarvis had her car packed, a term paper turned in, and was heading home.

Bud Davis stood close by the grave and cried through the part where most people would've padded the quiet with hymns. Dorilee had planned the service herself, long ago. And Dorilee Davis had never much been like most people.

With no warning from either the radio or the sky, it rained that day, great big walls of water collapsing onto the mourners' heads, utterly drenching them all—but anyone could still see Bud was crying.

The Mount Airy Episcopal minister stood to deliver the eulogy. On her deathbed, and very nearly her final words, Dorilee had said she didn't much care which of the town clergy did the eulogy but picked the Episcopalian as the most likely to use good grammar. She knew she couldn't rest, she said, if the final formal mention of her name on earth were in a sentence with subject-verb disagreement.

It was when the Episcopalian preacher finally finished saying nice, eloquent—grammatically correct—things about the corpse and when the undertakers, who'd heard it all before more or less, stopped leaning on their shovels, that Dorilee Davis's husband said, softly but audibly, "She was a good woman every day of her whole life long."

Arlene Veal glanced up, big eyed, looking first incredulous—then ashamed of looking incredulous. Her head dropped.

Jarvis found her own thoughts sliding back—for probably the first time in nine years—to that pediatrician's office with a nightmare of a nurse's aide who smelled of two kinds of alcohol. And to that young mother whose twelve-year-old, redheaded boy hung himself in his bedroom closet.

Arlene Veal may have been the anchorwoman on her university's TV news program, but just then with the rain running off that funny promontory of chin beneath a striking (though straight) nose, her wet hair dark and flat and parted in the middle, she looked, Jarvis couldn't help thinking, a whole lot like she did in sixth grade. For a moment, Jarvis was certain Arlene was going to make a face. Then Arlene Veal looked back down at the dirt instead.

"She was," Dorilee Davis's husband continued, "a perfect wife to me always."

Involuntarily, Jarvis cringed. She pulled her coat more tightly about herself and tried to drag her thoughts back from where they'd just leapt: old sports-page clippings of a woman tall and slender and graceful with a racket—and other people's husbands. Jarvis searched for something to look at that wouldn't look back. Directly across from her, Rusty Cotter, whose plane from Newark had been delayed, was still breathing hard, having run from where the taxi let him off clear across the cemetery. She could pick him out without looking for his face: his pants all spattered now in Tennessee clay, a heavy trim of thick, dripping orange at the hem of stiff, dark blue jeans—all in one piece, even the knees.

Freddy Hawkins's kids were there, every last one

of the pack, though the dog, Jarvis had heard, had died last winter. They all had shoes on their feet and were all fully clothed, looking pink cheeked and bright eyed and standing almost still; it occurred to Jarvis that Freddy must be doing all right now. Freddy himself was there, wiping his eyes, then his nose, then his eyes again.

Jarvis looked up just long enough to see that no one else was looking up. They were all studying the dirt.

"That's all she wanted," said Dorilee Davis's husband, choking a little on his own breath, which was coming quickly and sporadically, full of moisture, with a moan caught somewhere down too deep to escape. "That's all she wanted on her marker," he said, and he wept.

They all stood, still saying nothing, staring at the grave marker the deceased had chosen herself: a granite rock with one side planed flat—no lilies, no urns, no angels—not even her name. Not even her date of birth. Or death. Just these words: "Yet in my flesh I shall see God."

When he'd called Jarvis about Dorilee's dying and about the funeral, Bud Davis had mentioned the marker. Though barely able to make himself understood, he seemed to want Jarvis to know it hadn't been his idea: no stinginess on his part, the grave marker without so much as her name, not even her first name—not even that. "That's all she wanted on it," he'd said miserably over the phone.

In living, Dorilee wasn't always a reasonable woman, Jarvis knew, and she tried to find a way to say that, gently, to Bud. So who could blame the deceased if she was a little difficult about her own death?

"That's all she wanted," Bud said once more by the grave, lifting his head slowly until the gray crew cut was level, and looking at them, the little crowd gathered there, with the eyes of a small boy left alone in a storm. It was only then they realized he'd been asking a question.

They huddled closer to him then, and Jarvis felt the rain making its way through her hair and underneath the up-turned collar of her wool coat and down her back. Together they all stood there in the storm and shivered while the rain soaked them through, and their breath came out in puffs of mist and mingled with the fog—until they could tell by his face that Dorilee Davis's husband had his answer.

Jarvis placed a little pot of petunias on the grave,

beside the marker without a name, without a date, not even an angel or an urn. Arlene Veal took one of Bud's arms; Jarvis took the other—and together the little group by the grave walked Dorilee Davis's husband home.

Jarvis Darby looked back only once—to see the little pot of petunias sitting there in the rain, watered well.

I Should Have, Could Have, Used to, Still

I should have,
  you know,
    Should have what, dear?
Should have gone to Africa. I meant to,
  you know.
    But I thought you sold—
Signed all the college yearbooks "Bound for Africa."
    Downtown, wasn't it? What you actually did was—
Worked for Sears instead.
    Ah. You were right then: "Bound for Sears" has a different ring.
It's okay. I'm eighty-nine and counting. They pay a good retirement now.

I could have,
  you know.

Could have what, dear?
Could have married. I meant to,
  you know.
    Married? You? Not that you're hard to live with, mind you.
Asked to many times.
    How many is many?
Didn't realize the last time was . . . the last time.
    Ah. Last time. Guess there had to be one.
It's okay. I'm eighty-nine and counting. I've outlived them all now.

I used to,
  you know.
    Used to what, dear?
Shake a wicked leg. I went dancing often,
  you know.
    And a wicked *leg was what you shook, was it?*
There were those who thought me good.
    Then why . . . ?
Joined the Baptist church, and back then . . .
    Ah. Baptist. Say no more.
It's okay. I'm eighty-nine and counting. I've got a busted hip now.

I still do,
  you know.

Still do what, dear?

Still enjoy the company of young men. Handsome ones, you understand.

Yes. I've noticed.

Republicans, preferably. And tall.

Ah. Tall. Republicans. And young.

Handsome, you understand. But I'm not hard to please, you know.

You?

It's okay. I'm eighty-nine and counting. They think I'm awfully cute now.

Crusader in Floral Print

At ninety-five, Rose Phillips cannot walk up the stairs. In fact, to watch her now, one wonders if she ever ascended steps like the rest of us: one foot slowly pulleyed up behind the other.

Rose Phillips *charges:* up stairs, across platforms, and into prisons. Elbows out, fists rounded, arms bent and pumping her forward, she moves like a marathoner who has never yet stopped short of the finish line. Rose attends to life with an utterly unswerving single-mindedness. Attempt to distract her at your own risk. Thoroughbreds wearing blinders never ran a course so straight.

Whatever she does, wherever she goes, she is a woman on a mission. Her armor typically takes the form of a floral-print dress—but any image of petal-like fragility belies the steel of the Rose underneath.

A magazine once asked me to write a feature on Rose. *Sure,* I thought. *Rose Phillips is my friend, known her for years.* I already had the litany of her talents memorized: Poet, Painter, Pianist, Preacher. How hard could this be?

Never try to write about anyone three times your age who can outrun you.

In the role of reporter, I followed her to the medium-security men's prison where she preaches every month *and* provides poetry *and* paints the cover of the service programs: prison parson . . . picked a peck of pickled peppers. I was already beginning to scribble some notes: a sure sign I was feeling good about the piece. I'd be done writing by dinner.

At the prison's main entrance, Rose submitted—an event in itself—to having her belongings searched (women nearly a century old and five feet tall apparently being likely candidates for aiding and abetting jail breaks).

In the dining hall the inmates sang while awaiting their leader, their amplifiers rattling the concrete-block walls. Rose walked in and took charge, and men who'd committed grand larceny, second-degree murder, and manslaughter turned meek and compliant. Rose slowed the tempo to a series of statelier melodies. Prisoners of more upbeat tastes remained undaunted, cheerfully pounding out revival tunes on bongos, maracas, and electric guitars. Rose kept time on the metal podium with one hand and alternately snapped the fingers of the other.

I added Percussionist to my list.

Then, in quick transition from the last song to a sermon, she strode to the podium. With a personal presence that makes a just-over-five-foot frame tower over her audience, she held the microphone close to her mouth. Each word had been carefully chosen and now was carefully, forcefully uttered. I put three stars by Pulpiteer.

One inmate hustled up after the closing hymn to thump Rose affectionately—and rather hard—on the back. Grinning good-naturedly, she thumped him—rather hard—on the shoulder. "God gives her strength," he said to me. "I'm twenty-eight and I look forty. She's ninety something and looks younger than I do." I started to write Well Preserved but decided against it.

Burly men with tattoos soon flocked around the preacher in the floral-print dress to give her news of their lives. She listened with parental interest.

And somewhere in the course of her preaching and her interaction with the prison inmates, her parishioners, Rose revealed—without ever mentioning herself—the secret of her own endurance.

Like a divinely powered Energizer rabbit, Rose manages to, as she puts it, "keep on keeping on," even through life's disabling setbacks. Born in 1901 in Cambridge, Massachusetts, of Armenian descent, Rose Phillips (*Phillips* an Americanization of *Pillobossian*) could speak no English when she first began school. When she was sixteen her mother died. As the oldest of three children, Rose cared for her siblings.

I penciled in Primary Care-Giver/ Principal Income.

Squeezed in among pressing duties, she attended college and seminary, receiving a ministerial degree. For the next ten years, which included World War II and the resulting gas rations, Rose motored throughout New England as an itinerant evangelist: preaching, leading seminars—whatever was needed. For this she received twenty dollars a month. A few more dollars, a very few, came from her position as assistant pastor of a Baptist congregation in Cambridge, Massachusetts. She emphasized the *assistant* part. I underlined the *P* in Pastor: I bet I knew who was in charge.

"I've always lived frugally," she explained, adding that she began sewing her own clothes at age twelve. "What would I have done with more money?" She didn't wait for suggestions. "Give it away," she said.

I wrote down Pauper, then crossed it out. I suspect she's never missed the money.

Adequate income or not, Rose kept on keeping on. At one point, doctors discovered she had breast cancer. A mastectomy but no chemotherapy followed. But don't bother thinking Cancer Patient: that was four decades ago.

Then came Boston's infamous blizzard of 1978. As Rose was trekking to church through the snow, someone from a passing car grabbed her bag (containing exactly, she likes to recount, two saucers, two cups, and eight slices of bread). Maintaining her grip on the bag (whether out of reflex or plain old stubbornness, she cannot say), Rose was dragged under the moving car. A rear wheel ran over her leg and elbow. "I thought I'd pretty well fallen off the trolley that time," she chuckled. Though her skin was split open, fifteen x-rays revealed not one broken bone. I began writing Pretty Well Fallen . . . , but stopped to calculate her age at the time: seventy-seven. Nearly twenty years ago. I moved on to the next line.

At ninety-five Rose Phillips insists on remaining in the apartment that has been her home since youth—even though it sits atop three flights of narrow, winding stairs. Five years ago when she fell and broke two ribs, Rose's doctor insisted she restrain activity. Friends offered to install a door-unlatching system that would save her the three-flight hike up and down to admit visitors. One friend offered rappelling gear. She would hear none of it. Particularly Hard-Headed, I was tempted to write, but didn't because she could see me writing.

Three weeks ago, Rose Phillips fell again, breaking another rib and fracturing her spine. This time a young doctor wisely noted that the physical activity necessitated by where—and how—Rose insists on living has actually contributed to her continued health and agility all these years. Medical Science Meets Rose Phillips . . . and finds she's beaten them there.

The day after her fall, I paid Rose a visit. Standing on the stoop of her house, I fumbled in my briefcase for the get-well card I'd brought her—searching for it amongst Kleenex, half-graded Freshman Composition papers, bills to mail and mail to read, and a baby rattle—when Rose lowered the front-door key down on a string suspended from the third floor. I let myself in and barely had time to release the key as Rose was already retrieving the string. I leveraged myself up the staircase, which heels to one side like a sailboat in strong wind.

I see Rose regularly, but it had been awhile since I'd been in her home. Her apartment is simple: linoleum floor seams smoothed with electrical tape, all the furniture practical, functional. Everything is labeled. Everything. Even a cluster of bud vases on a separate shelf that looks fairly self-explanatory. I think of my study at home: ankle deep in manuscripts in mid-revision and research notes on medieval literature; cardboard, cocked sideways, secured to the computer screen with excessive strips of masking tape, blocks the morning sun; a hand-me-down playpen sits conspicuously at the hub of the room, powerfully symbolic of attention that is never undivided these days.

I watched Rose scoot across her kitchen floor to find the letter she wanted to show me from a mutual friend in California. No searching. It is, naturally, exactly where it should be. *How do you do that?* I felt like shouting at her.

Her strength—of body and of will—derives from a daily ritual conducted at an hour that makes the rising sun look slothful. Awake each morning by four, Rose lies still, praying and meditating for the first two to four hours of her day. Having shared a not overly large apartment with a father and two brothers in the first decades of her life, she found her bed "a sanctuary, my only . . . privacy." Today, alone, having outlived all her family, Rose continues to honor her wee-hours tradition.

Afternoon provides time for painting: "my therapy," as she calls it, for which her bedroom turns art studio. Rose's artistic skills were spawned by necessity when her duties at a utility-company job required her to paint greeting cards. The apartment's only other bedroom has been permanently transformed into a combination gallery and art-storage closet. There, stack upon stack of New England coastline paintings and mountain landscapes—granite behemoths—line the walls and floors of the room.

Rose Phillips herself has something of the look of granite about her. It still takes me by surprise when she smiles, her whole face going warm and friendly, occasionally even playful.

It was her artistic talent, a still-steady soprano voice, and her abilities as a pianist that relatives—and she herself at one time—hoped would provide a lucrative career. Though ultimately becoming nei-ther a professional painter nor a musician, she is quick to point out, "My gifts have been used for a higher purpose." She still leads a monthly community program and co-leads a nursing home worship service, playing piano and preaching at both—for "the elderly," she calls them.

Given what she does with her days, it's not surprising that a large portion of Cambridge, Massachusetts, knows Rose. And a large portion of those who move on from there keep in touch with her. Her last birthday brought greetings from friends in Austria and Arizona, Hong Kong and Hamburg, Taipei and Texas.

Rose Phillips: Public Figure, Pal.

While acknowledging the part she has played in the transformation of so many lives, Rose accepts all compliments as a park ranger might acknowledge applause for a particularly stunning sunset: it's God at work. No room for either arrogance or false humility.

"Someone stopped me today to say," she recently told me, "that when he heard me preach, he felt himself in the presence of *greatness*." She threw her head back then and had a good, hard laugh, adding,

"I think he was a little, you know, not entirely *there.*"

Rose has lived all her adult life single and celibate. "I've never had time to be lonely," she will tell you, looking as though she harbors grave doubts about those who do. "And I wouldn't allow myself to become depressed. It would be an insult to God. It's just a matter of rising above circumstances, a matter of realizing that God is able."

Rose Phillips is ferocious in clarifying the source of her strength and her sense of mission. And she refuses to be admired apart from what she stands for. Get it wrong at your peril.

Poet, Painter, Preacher, and Pianist. Paragon. Powerhouse. And . . . Pilgrim. The feature article I'd been asked to write was clearly going to be more difficult than I'd first envisioned, trying to put this . . . Phenomenon . . . down on paper. Because Rose Phillips's life has its own beat—and knowing her, she probably made the drum herself from little things around the house. Things that were carefully labeled.

In the role of reporter, at our final official interview (in the basement of her church), I had more questions to ask, lots more. But Rose Phillips, who had noticed her ride home waiting, had already kissed my cheek, bid me good night and *charged* up the stairs before I could put down my pen.

Never try to write about anyone three times your age who—with a broken rib—can outrun you.

For Pelvis Wide and Tears We've Cried

Lately, I've slowed down—quite against my will, I might add. I've been listening to my own life and to the lives of the people around me, with all their scratch and clatter and riffs and trills. There is much noise about the music we make in living, you and I, much noise and much nonsense.

But the God of peace and purpose insists we lift our voices over the music and the noise . . . and give thanks. Not to glibly offer thanks for all things—that would be naive and insincere and deadly dishonest. Glibness always shrinks from the stark light of real life's bare bulb: the still-wet hair of a stillborn baby, the clenched hand of a pain-wracked loved one, marriage vows that come unraveled from the careless stitches of inattention. . . . There are times when we meet life with our arms outstretched only to find it coming at us fanged and ferocious.

Sometimes, though . . . sometimes there is, for those who look, beauty lying buried somewhere in the ashes; sometimes a rose still blooms amidst the rubble, deep, deep down under. Sometimes. And sometimes we can help each other find humor in the crazy quilt patterns of our chaotic lives. Sometimes, too, we can remind each other—and ourselves—that there are lessons that can only be learned in a storm. So . . . ț 188

185

Let us give thanks
for skin that is new and soft,
sweet-smelling of cornstarch, milk
breath, wet kisses from Grandma and
the grocery-store cashier.
    But let us give thanks, too,
for skin that is tired, collapsing
finally in small folds and dry, gentle
pleats that speak of privilege: of many
days invested well.

Let us give thanks
for love's unloosed handsprings
that make us quiver and squeal, carve
initials on tree trunks, promise rashly to honor,
and always to hope.
    But let us give thanks, too,
for the high-walled limits of human love
that send us groping into hollow places, waste-
lands of our own resources, making us search
    again
for home.

Let us give thanks
for youth and agility, flexibility,
bodies in peak condition, for innocence still
far from experience, for tummies tight, bones
sturdy, all in line.
    But let us give thanks, too,
for stretch marks and sprung rib cages
and violently widened pelvic bones (never quite
snapped back): life expanding as it is lived, gaining
value given away.

Let us give thanks
for friends who stick around,
the next desk over, the last house down
the street, to share caffe latte and dreams too
outlandish to utter out loud.
    But let us give thanks, too,
for friends' waves from U-Haul truck
windows, leaving fumes and choked tears
in their wake, wrenching their roots from ours,
reminding both how we've grown.

Let us give thanks
for goals achieved and dreams come
true, for diplomas procured and jobs secured,
for big wins and standing ovations: admiration in
spotlights directed our way.
     But let us give thanks, too,
for noteworthy feats of remarkable
mediocrity, for outrageous failures, magnificent
flops—when they prod and pound us on
    towards . . .
better, much better, next time.

     Let us give thanks
for good health and vitality,
great energy, toned cardiovascular
systems, cool foreheads, warm feet, for endurance
to run well, run far.
     But let us give thanks, too,
for sinuses stopped solid, throats swollen shut
and migraines like meat cleavers on skulls—when
ailments release us to rest, scan for meaning,
to cease from reckless pursuit of the wind.

     Let us give thanks
for the parts of our physical selves
we need not conceal, lift, diminish, accentuate,
flatten—parts we might list as assets—but
won't.
     But let us give thanks, too,
for physical flaws: for broken-out skin
and thighs too thick, for teeth too crooked, thin
hair too straight—when we're reminded to
    makeover
our spirits, our minds.

     Let us give thanks
for green traffic lights on the way to work and
well-salted curves in winter, for fan belts properly
knowing their place, for tires' tread still apparent,
and traffic jams—in the opposite lane.
     But let us give thanks, too,
for parking meters we forget to feed, for
the speed limit signs we neglect to heed—when
they remind us to be grateful: for at least, at last,
today, the car did start.

Let us give thanks
for holidays and Sabbath days
for days of rest and peace, for breakfast out and
leisure hours, watches left behind, for hammocks
strung from hemlocks, swimsuits on the line.
    But let us give thanks, too,
for deadlines and for duties piled up to
drooping eyelids, for too-long days, so-late nights,
for pressures and stresses and last-minute faxes—
when hard work is finished well.

    Let us give thanks
for soaring leaps of faith exploring,
for gentle landings in our understanding
of this mystery: for feeling out the face of God,
for dancing on the deep.
    But let us give thanks, too,
for logical tumbles and stumbles of reason,
hearts and minds in high-wire balancing acts:
fear falling not as the finish but a time to start
    over
and take the teacher's hand.

So . . .
let us live with passion
in our everyday ploddings,
a discernible peace when the thunder rolls long;
let us mourn for our losses with arms linked
    together;
let us laugh at ourselves, urge each other up
    higher;
let us dance; let us grieve; tell our stories,
our tears; and when we recall
days of grace, . . . give
Thanks.

Books in the **WHEATON LITERARY SERIES:**

And It Was Good: Reflections on Beginnings, by Madeleine L'Engle. Cloth, 216 pages.

At a Theater Near You: Screen Entertainment from a Christian Perpective, by Thomas Patterson. Trade paper, 216 pages.

A Cry Like a Bell, poems by Madeleine L'Engle. Trade paper, 120 pages.

The Heart of George MacDonald: A One-Volume Collection of His Most Important Fiction, Essays, Sermons, Drama, and Biographical Information, edited by Rolland Hein. Cloth, 448 pages.

How to Read Slowly: Reading for Comprehension, by James W. Sire. Trade paper, 192 pages.

The Liberated Imagination: Thinking Christianly about the Arts, by Leland Ryken. Trade paper, 283 pages.

Life Essential: The Hope of the Gospel, by George MacDonald, edited by Rolland Hein. Trade paper, 104 pages.

Love Letters, fiction by Madeleine L'Engle. Cloth, 304 pages.

Maker & Craftsman: The Story of Dorothy L. Sayers, by Alzina Stone Dale. Trade paper, 172 pages.

Orthodoxy, by G. K. Chesterton. Cloth, 188 pages.

The Other Side of the Sun, fiction by Madeleine L'Engle. Cloth, 384 pages.

Penguins and Golden Calves: Icons and Idols by Madeleine L'Engle. Cloth, 192 pages.

Polishing the Petoskey Stone, poems by Luci Shaw. Cloth, 276 pages.

Postcard from the Shore, poems by Luci Shaw. Trade paper, 95 pages.

Realms of Gold: The Classics in Christian Perspective, by Leland Ryken. Trade paper, 240 pages.

The Rock that Is Higher: Story as Truth, by Madeleine L'Engle. Cloth, 296 pages.

The Sighting, poems by Luci Shaw. Trade paper, 95 pages.

Sold into Egypt: Joseph's Journey into Human Being, by Madeleine L'Engle. Cloth, 240 pages.

A Stone for a Pillow: Journeys with Jacob, by Madeleine L'Engle. Cloth, 240 pages.

T. S. Eliot: The Philosopher Poet, by Alzina Stone Dale. Cloth, 209 pages.

Walking on Water: Reflections on Faith and Art, by Madeleine L'Engle. Trade paper, 198 pages.

The Weather of the Heart, poems by Madeleine L'Engle. Trade paper, 96 pages.

WinterSong: Christmas Readings, by Madeleine L'Engle and Luci Shaw. Cloth, 208 pages.

Available from your local bookstore or from Harold Shaw Publishers, Box 567, Wheaton, IL 60189, 1-800-SHAWPUB